WITHDRAWN
From the
Dean B. Ellis Library
Arkansas State University

DEAN B. ELLIS LIBRARY

Columbia University

Contributions to Education

Teachers College Series

No. 613

AMS PRESS
NEW YORK

Indefinite Teacher Tenure

A Critical Study of the Historical, Legal, Operative, and Comparative Aspects

By CECIL WINFIELD SCOTT, Ph.D.

TEACHERS COLLEGE, COLUMBIA UNIVERSITY
CONTRIBUTIONS TO EDUCATION, NO. 613

*Published with the Approval of
Professor* WILLARD S. ELSBREE, *Sponsor*

BUREAU OF PUBLICATIONS
Teachers College, Columbia University
NEW YORK CITY
1934

Library of Congress Cataloging in Publication Data

Scott, Cecil Winfield, 1905-
  Indefinite teacher tenure.

  Reprint of the 1934 ed., issued in series:
Teachers College, Columbia University. Contributions
to education, no. 613.
  Originally presented as the author's thesis,
Columbia.
  Bibliography: p.
  1. Teachers--Tenure--United States. I. Title.
II. Series: Columbia University. Teachers College.
Contributions to education, no. 613.
LB2836.S3 1972   331.2'596   78-177799
ISBN 0-404-55613-2

Reprinted by Special Arrangement with Teachers
College Press, New York, New York

From the edition of 1934, New York
First AMS edition published in 1972
Manufactured in the United States

AMS PRESS, INC.
NEW YORK, N. Y.   10003

ACKNOWLEDGMENTS

To Professor Willard S. Elsbree, who suggested this study and whose wise counsel aided greatly in its execution, the writer is deeply indebted. He is also grateful to Professor I. L. Kandel, who assisted particularly with the comparative education phases of the investigation, and to Professors J. R. McGaughy and Carter Alexander, whose advice and criticism contributed much to the elevation of the quality of the final product.

For aid in collection of necessary data, the writer is indebted to officials of state departments of education and of state teachers' associations in the indefinite tenure states, to certain city school officials, to the National Education Association, the American Federation of Teachers, the National Civil Service Reform League, and the American Consul Generals in Germany, Italy, and Norway. The assistance of librarians and library workers of Teachers College and the Law School of Columbia University is also gratefully acknowledged.

Finally, the writer wishes to express his appreciation to fellow-students and friends outside the field of education, who generously gave of their time to discuss issues and procedures and a few of whom rendered most valuable aid in the translation of foreign materials.

C. W. S.

CONTENTS

CHAPTER	PAGE
I. INTRODUCTION	1
The Problem	2
Definition of Terms	3
Need for This Study	3
Limitation of the Problem	5
Method of Procedure	6
Selected References	8
II. DEVELOPMENT OF INDEFINITE TEACHER TENURE LEGISLATION	9
Relation of the Civil Service to Indefinite Tenure	9
Comparison of Civil Service and Indefinite Tenure Laws	10
Activities and Influence of the National Education Association	13
The American Federation of Teachers and Indefinite Tenure	16
Rôle of State Teachers' Associations	17
Chronological Review of Indefinite Tenure Legislation	22
Summary	24
Selected References	25
III. ANALYSIS AND EVALUATION ACCORDING TO ESTABLISHED CRITERIA OF EXISTING INDEFINITE TENURE LAWS	27
Analysis	27
Evaluation	41
Criteria	41
Application of Criteria	45
Summary	47
Selected References	48
IV. OPERATION OF INDEFINITE TEACHER TENURE LAWS	50
Evaluation of Major Claims for Indefinite Tenure	50
Dismissal of Undesirable Teachers	51
Protection from Unjustified Attacks and Anxiety Regarding Retention	53
Stabilization of the Profession	53
Drawing Power of Profession and Professional Improvement of Teachers	54
Certain Other Indefinite Tenure Problems	54
Probationary Periods	55
Rural Teacher Problem	55
Transfers and Resignations	56
Salary and Retirement Policies	57
Miscellaneous Problems	58
Tenure and Related Cases Arising Under the Illinois and New Jersey Laws	59
Chicago, Illinois	59

Contents

CHAPTER	PAGE
New Jersey	62
Summary	67
Selected References	69

V. OPERATION OF EXISTING STATE INDEFINITE TEACHER TENURE
LAWS AS REVEALED BY APPEAL CASES 70
Composite Data 70
Constitutionality of Indefinite Tenure Laws.............. 74
Purpose, or Theory, Underlying Indefinite Tenure Laws 75
Eligibility Requirements for Tenure Protection 77
Legal Interpretation of Major Protections Afforded Teachers . 78
    Summary Dismissal 79
    Manner of Preferring Charges and Nature Thereof 79
    Hearing Requirement and Its Nature 80
    Appeal Rights and Procedures 81
Power of Local Boards Under Indefinite Teacher Tenure Laws 85
Questions of Probation 87
    Purpose of Probation 87
    Dismissal of Probationary Teachers 88
    Length of Probationary Period and Reckoning Thereof ... 89
    Place of Service 92
    Rôle of Contract and of Board Action in Initiating Tenure
        Protection 92
    Effect of Promotion upon Teacher Status 94
Cases Involving Administrative Problems of Transfer, Abolition
of Position, Suspension, Resignation, and Salary Reduction . 95
    Transfer Cases 95
    Abolition of Position 98
    Suspension 99
    Resignation 100
    Salary Reduction 101
Cases Arising Largely from Dismissal Following Charges 103
    Inefficiency and Incompetency 103
    Incapacity 105
    Unbecoming Conduct 106
    Unprofessional Conduct 108
    Other Just Cause 109
    Insubordination 110
    Miscellaneous 110
Selected References 112

VI. COMPARISON OF TEACHER TENURE AND CERTAIN RELATED
ASPECTS OF TEACHER PERSONNEL REGULATIONS AND PRACTICES IN SIX EUROPEAN COUNTRIES WITH SIMILAR PROVISIONS
AND CONDITIONS EXISTING IN THE AMERICAN STATES HAVING
INDEFINITE TENURE LAWS 114
Training of Teachers 116
    Elementary Teachers 117
    Secondary Teachers 121

Contents

CHAPTER	PAGE
Appointments, Probationary Periods, and Transfers	124
Appointments	125
Probationary Requirements and Practices	127
Transfers	130
Tenure and Disciplinary Regulations and Practices	131
Tenure	131
Discipline	133
Salary and Pension Provisions	137
Summary	137
Selected References	139
VII. SUMMARY OF OUTCOMES AND RECOMMENDATIONS FOR INDEFINITE TENURE AND RELATED LEGISLATION	141
Summary	141
Recommendations	144
Related Laws	145
Administrative Units	145
Certification	146
Retirement	146
Salaries	147
Indefinite Tenure Laws	147
General Recommendations	147
Application to Districts	148
Application to Employees	148
Classification of Educational Employees	149
Type of Tenure	150
Probationary Regulations	150
Disciplinary Regulations	151
Disciplinary Authority	151
Scale of Penalties	151
Suspension	151
Dismissal	151
Disciplinary Procedure	152
Charges	152
Hearings	152
Notices	152
Appeals	152
Transfers	153
Resignations	153
Salaries	153
In-Service Training	154
Conclusion	154
GENERAL BIBLIOGRAPHY	155
APPENDIX	
A. APPEAL CASES THAT HAVE ARISEN UNDER EXISTING INDEFINITE TEACHER TENURE LAWS LISTED ACCORDING TO TYPE	159
B. ABBREVIATIONS FOR LEGAL SOURCES	165

TABLES

TABLE		PAGE
I.	Comparison of the Dates of Enactment of State Civil Service Laws and Indefinite Teacher Tenure Laws	10
II.	Application of Indefinite Teacher Tenure Laws, Educational Qualifications for Protection Thereunder, and Probationary Periods Provided	28
III.	Suspension and Dismissal Provisions of Indefinite Tenure Laws for Discipline of Permanent Teachers	30
IV.	Causes for Dismissal, Manner of Preferring Charges, and Nature of Hearing Provided in Indefinite Tenure Laws	33
V.	Appeal Procedures for Dismissed Teachers Provided in Existing Indefinite Tenure Laws	36
VI.	Provisions for Resignation in Existing Indefinite Tenure Laws	38
VII.	Miscellaneous Provisions of Existing Indefinite Tenure Laws	39
VIII.	Application of Criteria to Existing Indefinite Teacher Tenure Laws	46
IX.	Teacher Dismissal Cases Occurring in Chicago from 1920–1931, Inclusive	60
X.	Minor Teacher Disciplinary Cases in Chicago, 1920–1931, Inclusive, and Disposition Thereof	61
XI.	Types of Cases and Corresponding Numbers of Each Considered by the Committee on Grievances and Redress of the New Jersey State Teachers' Association from 1926–1931, Inclusive	64
XII.	Appeal Cases with Dicisions Thereon That Have Arisen under the Several State Indefinite Teacher Tenure Laws from the Dates of Passage through 1931	71
XIII.	Distribution of Appeal Cases Arising under State Indefinite Teacher Tenure Laws According to Final Ruling Authority and Decisions Rendered	72
XIV.	Distribution of Indefinite Teacher Tenure Appeal Cases for California, Massachusetts, New Jersey, and New York According to Final Ruling Authority and Decisions Rendered	73
XV.	Chronological Distribution of Appeal Cases Arising under the Several State Indefinite Teacher Tenure Laws from the Respective Dates of Passage Through 1931	74
XVI.	Minimum Training Requirements for Teaching in Terms of College Years Operating in States Having Indefinite Tenure Laws, June 1932	117

CHAPTER I

Introduction

CONSIDERABLE controversy has centered about the question of indefinite tenure since its entrance into the arena of public education and as yet unanimity of opinion with regard to the matter does not exist either among members of the educational profession or of the lay public. Affirmatively, it has been held that teachers need protection against designing politicians and that such protection would naturally result in an improved profession and thus in better schools. Negatively, claims have been made that protection in office causes teachers to lose interest in self-betterment and therefore tends either to maintain the *status quo* or even to retard progress. Studies thus far made of the problem have established no scientific bases for either position; and it is doubtful whether scientific research can ever settle the issue, since it is so difficult to segregate and measure the results of indefinite tenure, except for the single feature of protection. Hence the matter becomes one for acceptance or rejection on the basis of governmental policy or social philosophy. It might well be argued that any governmental unit should grant tenure protection to its teachers since they, more than any other group of government employees or citizens, can contribute to its perpetuation. This position is defensible; but the social justice theory is more in keeping with trends of thought in regard to human relationships, especially as these assume legal form in the field of social jurisprudence.

Indefinite teacher tenure naturally falls in the category with old age pensions, retirement annuities, workmen's compensation acts, unemployment insurance, and other types of social legislation, although strictly speaking it is not social legislation. All such laws are aimed at protecting the individual against unjust treatment from the forces of society to which he is subject. Their underlying philosophy is in all cases the same. And it is on the basis of this philosophy that they can be best supported, one and all. The principle of indefinite tenure, then, appears to merit the support of all socially-minded individuals. With the instruments designed for applying the principle, i.e., indefinite tenure laws, the case is rather different. These devices may vary from over-protection of teachers through proper safeguarding of all interests involved to over-protection of the schools, or at least to too little security for teachers. In 1879 President Charles W. Eliot declared that

If public opinion settles down upon the conviction that a tenure for teachers during good behavior and efficiency is expedient and desirable, some legal way of attaining what is desirable will be found or made.[1]

Laws have been enacted; yet it is a patent fact that in a number of respects they have failed to produce the desired ends. The province of this study is to examine carefully the provisions and operation of existing laws with a view to proposing suggestions for their improvement and for the drafting of other laws.

THE PROBLEM

Primarily, the purpose of this investigation is to ascertain what provisions should make up an indefinite tenure law or what guiding principles should control the framing of one that aims at the greatest possible protection of the interests of all groups concerned, namely, those of teachers, children, and society in general. A secondary purpose, to be achieved as a by-product of the major one, is that of tracing the development of indefinite tenure laws and of presenting information concerning the provisions of existing statutes and their operation. These facts will help students of the subject and educators in general to clarify their thinking relative to the issues involved and will acquaint teachers with their rights under protective tenure laws. The major problem is divided into six minor ones as follows:

1. To trace the development of indefinite teacher tenure laws and to show the most important factors responsible for their growth, with actuating motives.

2. To analyze existing laws and to evaluate them in terms of criteria commonly accepted among educators when the laws were enacted.

3. To identify a majority of the fundamental problems of indefi-

[1] Eliot, Charles W., "Teachers' Tenure of Office"; In *Educational Reform*, p. 49.

Introduction

nite tenure and to evaluate critically the common claims made for the practice—this to be accomplished through a study of operative effects of present laws, as shown by published comments, former research studies, and several case studies.

4. To identify problems further and to exhibit the legal aspects of the operation of existing statutes through a study of cases of appeal from dismissal.

5. To set forth the main provisions for teacher tenure and closely related personnel regulations and procedures in six European countries and to compare these conditions with corresponding facts for the American states having indefinite tenure laws.

6. To develop recommendations for protective tenure and allied legislation, based upon the outcomes of the study.

DEFINITION OF TERMS

The term "indefinite tenure" is used herein to signify protection of teachers in office after completion of a probationary period. This term is preferable to "tenure," so commonly used, which covers all contractual relationships regardless of length, and to "permanent tenure" or "life tenure," both of which imply an unusually high degree of stability. Terms used in this study as synonymous with "indefinite tenure" are "safeguarded tenure," "protective tenure," and "security in office."

The word "teacher" as employed in this investigation signifies any educational employee who enjoys protection under an indefinite tenure statute. However, this does not preclude use of exact titles where such are either interesting or important.

NEED FOR THIS STUDY

One reason for this study, and the most important one, is that a number of American states now have indefinite tenure laws which need to be revised and that the trend is toward enactment of additional laws. Twelve states now have statutes which apply either generally or in restricted areas; these states are California, Colorado, Illinois, Indiana, Louisiana, Maryland, Massachusetts, Minnesota, New Jersey, New York, Oregon, Wisconsin.[2] The District of Columbia also has a statute and since it affects as many teachers

[2] For dates of enactment, see Table I, Chap. II; and for provisions, see Chap. III.

as do a few of the state laws, and because it was one of the first to be enacted, this statute is included in the study. Continuing contract laws are found in three states; the Montana and Nevada laws are state-wide, while the Pennsylvania law applies to all districts except those of the first class.[3] Ohio has a law applying to all districts which permits contracts for more than one year and the following other states have such laws applying in certain districts: Mississippi, Nebraska, North Dakota, Texas (*supra*[3]). The continuing contract has been defined as "a plan whereby teachers may hold their positions without the necessity of annual applications, elections, and contracts."[4] It provides for automatic reëmployment after a specified date each year, provided neither party has given notice prior thereto of discontinuance of the contract. Obviously, the continuing contract and the permissive contract laws are steps toward indefinite tenure. Another indication of the trend mentioned above is that a number of states have tried unsuccessfully to pass protective tenure laws during the past decade, this fact being established definitely for Georgia, Nebraska, Ohio, Oklahoma, Pennsylvania, and West Virginia. Perhaps more important yet is the current tendency to set up legal protections for the individual against economic and social forces beyond his control. As one of such protections, indefinite tenure laws will very likely increase in number. Consequently, a comprehensive study of indefinite tenure, one which throws into relief legal aspects, should be of value not only for revision purposes but also for use in the framing of new statutes.

Another reason for this study is that no previous investigation has adequately covered certain phases of the field, namely, the historical, the purely legal, and the comparative. More studies of indefinite tenure have doubtless been made by the National Education Association, functioning through special committees, than by any other organization or by any individual.[5] What appears to be the most important report of the Association was issued in 1924.[6] The main contents of this study are: analysis of existing state laws, survey of local indefinite tenure regulations, survey

---

[3] *Report of the Committee of One Hundred on Tenure Problems of the N.E.A.*, 1932, p. 5.

[4] *Ibid.*, p. 9.

[5] For details concerning the various reports, except for the one explained here, see Chap. II, pp. 13-15.

[6] "The Problem of Teacher Tenure," *N. E. A. Research Bul.*, Vol. 2, No. 5, Nov. 1924.

of tenure practices in certain European countries, development—on the basis of professional and lay opinion—of charges which justify dismissal of a teacher, and presentation of outstanding facts regarding some flagrant cases of political dismissal and of a few court cases that afforded the occasion for indefinite tenure legislation. This report is largely valuable for the picture it presents of indefinite tenure in the United States in 1924. A somewhat similar study is that of Vanatta,[7] completed in the same year, which analyzes both existing and proposed protective tenure laws, presents opinions of school superintendents and educational experts regarding indefinite tenure, and evolves a set of criteria for the framing of laws as well as a model statute. Holmstedt's study[8] of the operation of the New Jersey law, which compares teacher personnel conditions in New Jersey with those existent in Connecticut, a non-protective tenure state, where the teacher's contract period is ordinarily one year, is, in the writer's opinion, the best study in the field. Major outcomes of this investigation are that the New Jersey law has not reduced the amount of dismissal, but has merely caused it to occur earlier in the employment of teachers; that there is some evidence, although slight, that the New Jersey law has been a stabilizing factor; that teachers having protection show no greater or less interest in professional improvement than non-protected ones; and that protection is the chief value of the New Jersey law. Numerous cursory studies of the problem have been made and much has been written on the topic, but the value of these is not sufficient to warrant any specific details here.

LIMITATION OF THE PROBLEM

The most important limitation of this study is that it attempts in no way to prove the value or desirability of indefinite tenure. As has been pointed out, the principle has to be accepted or thrown aside on the basis of governmental policy or social philosophy. Provisions for statutes designed to put the principle into operation may, however, be evaluated on the basis of the effects they produce. This study concentrates attention on the instruments of indefinite tenure rather than on the concept itself.

[7] Vanatta, H. E., "A Study of Existing and Proposed Tenure Laws." In Ms. (1924).
[8] Holmstedt, Raleigh W., *A Study of the Effects of the Teacher Tenure Law in New Jersey.*

Other limitations of the investigation are these: (1) Intensive study is confined to indefinite tenure laws; continuous contract laws, local regulations for protective tenure, and other such provisions are not accepted as providing indefinite tenure. (2) Protection for educational employees in public schools is the only type considered. (3) The operation of existing laws is studied only through published comments, former research studies, a few case studies, and cases of appeal from dismissal. Appeal cases are restricted to those that have been decided by state educational authorities and by the Supreme and Appellate Courts. (4) Comparison of indefinite tenure conditions in this country with those of six European countries, England and Wales, France, Germany, Italy, Norway, and Sweden, is confined to the rudimentary facts concerning training requirements, procedure for appointment and transfer, tenure and discipline, and salary and pension regulations.

Three phases of this investigation offer opportunity for further study, namely, the historical development of indefinite tenure, the operation of existing laws, and tenure regulations and practices in European countries. The history of individual laws might be pursued to a greater extent and the tenure-promotive activities of professional associations other than those treated herein might be investigated with interest and profit. Intensive case studies of the operation of particular laws, such as the Holmstedt study of the New Jersey law (*supra*[8]) would be of value in determining the adequacy of present statutes.[9] A study of appeal cases that have been decided by county courts in California, Indiana, and Massachusetts might produce worth-while results. Finally, more detailed studies of teacher tenure and related personnel regulations and practices in the major European countries would very likely yield returns of significance to the administration of teacher personnel in this country.

METHOD OF PROCEDURE

Earlier research studies, published articles on the subject, news notes, and the literature of civil service furnished the bulk of the information used in the historical treatment and in the development of criteria for evaluating existing laws; these sources also

[9] A Master's thesis study of the Indiana law was being made in 1932 by L. T. Stafford, Indianapolis Public Schools, Indianapolis, Ind.

contributed an appreciable proportion of the facts regarding operation. For the analysis of statutes now in force, copies of the latest school codes were obtained from the various state departments of education and the aid of these departments was enlisted in segregating tenure sections, in interpreting doubtful points, and in ferreting out related provisions of the law. Originally it was planned to study intensively the operation of two state laws, i.e., those of New Jersey and New York, through the means of board records of personnel administration in selected cities in each state, but this procedure proved to be too unproductive. A thorough case study of the operation of the Illinois law (which applies only to Chicago) for a twelve-year period, was made possible through the availability of Proceedings of the Board of Education of Chicago at Teachers College, Columbia University. The New Jersey law was studied by means of records covering a period of six years of the Committee on Grievances and Redress of the State Teachers' Association. These two case studies are the most important ones made; however, information was collected from several cities by means of correspondence and personal visitation.

Since the study of appeal cases covers all such cases as have been decided by higher educational and legal authorities since the several laws went into effect, the first task here was to find the cases. References appearing in former researches were recorded; a search was made under appropriate headings in the American Digest System[10] for cases finally settled by legal tribunals; and, finally, some state departments were asked to furnish lists of cases and all departments represented checked for completeness the final lists prepared by the writer. It is believed that this method resulted in the accumulation of all existent cases. Once collected, the cases were read and either digested or annotated. Then followed the presentation of this information in a write-up which, after giving summary data for the cases, shows how the various statutes have been interpreted by ruling authorities. This treatment reveals, largely by inference, good and bad features of the various laws.

The literature of comparative education furnished a considerable part of the information needed for the comparative study; but some material was obtained from the central authorities for

---

[10] This System claims to list under general headings and under cross references all cases decided in courts of record in the United States.

education in several of the countries studied, through the courtesy of the American consuls located in these countries.

Summarizing outcomes and developing recommendations for indefinite tenure legislation marked the final stage of the study. The recommendations are divided into two groups: (1) suggestions for accompanying legislation which should be in force before an indefinite tenure law is enacted; (2) recommendations for the content of an indefinite tenure section. No model law is set forth, since it is highly improbable that any one statute would meet the varying conditions and needs of the several states; but general and specific principles are enunciated which can be applied in any situation.

SELECTED REFERENCES

BEARD, CHARLES A. and M. R. *The Rise of American Civilization*, pp. 762-63. The Macmillan Company, New York, 1930.

CALCOTT, MARY STEVENSON. *Principles of Social Legislation*. The Macmillan Company, New York, 1932.

DAGGETT, H. S. "Developments in Law as a Social Science." *Journal of the Louisiana Teachers' Association*, 9:29-33, October 1931.

NATIONAL EDUCATION ASSOCIATION. *Report of the Committee of One Hundred on Tenure Problems of the National Education Association.* Washington, D. C., 1932.

CHAPTER II

Development of Indefinite Teacher Tenure Legislation

RELATION OF THE CIVIL SERVICE TO INDEFINITE TENURE

HISTORICAL evidence and careful consideration both lead to the conclusion that indefinite teacher tenure is an application, although a decidedly restricted one, of the civil service principle and that civil service legislation has considerably influenced legislation for the protection of teachers in office. Proponents of the latter have long held that teachers are in reality civil servants and, therefore, are entitled to protection similar to that afforded recognized members of the civil service. In an address on the tenure of office and maintenance of teachers delivered at the annual meeting of the National Education Association in 1885, Waite[1] classified teachers as members of the civil service, saying:

> Let it not be forgotten that the schools in which we train our citizens at the public expense, and the teachers employed in them under the provisions of our laws, are to be duly recognized in the complex machinery of our civic organism as among the active efficiencies which we vaguely describe as the "Civil Service."[1]

More recent statements in educational journals have frequently reiterated the claim that indefinite tenure is merely an application of the civil service idea to the schools. Teachers in European countries are, generally speaking, regarded as civil servants, having legal protection in their positions; but only twelve American states and the District of Columbia have accorded teachers in this country such legal recognition.

Proof that civil service legislation has influenced teacher tenure legislation consists entirely of the published statements referred to above and of the chronological records of the two types of laws showing when each type has been enacted by state governments and the District of Columbia. Table I presents a comparison of chronological facts. It is significant that eight of the ten states

---

[1] Waite, Henry Randall, "Civil Service Reform and the Public Schools . . . ," *N.E.A. Jl. of Proc. and Addresses*, 1885, Vol. 24, p. 122.

having state civil service laws also have indefinite tenure laws for teachers; that two others which have restricted civil service laws likewise have protective teacher tenure statutes; and that the District of Columbia, although it has but one type of legislation, ordinarily applies the merit principle in selection of its civil employees. Obviously, there are but two states each with but one of the two types of laws. More noteworthy than the facts just pointed out, however, is the fact that civil service statutes antedated teacher tenure legislation in all states having both types

TABLE I

COMPARISON OF THE DATES OF ENACTMENT OF STATE CIVIL SERVICE LAWS AND INDEFINITE TEACHER TENURE LAWS[1]

State	Civil Service	Indefinite Tenure
California	1913	1921
Colorado	1907	1921
District of Columbia	[2]	1906
Illinois	1905	1917
Indiana		1927
Kansas	1916[3]	
Louisiana		1922
Maryland	1920	1916
Massachusetts	1884	1914
Minnesota	1921[4]	1927
Ohio	1912	
New Jersey	1908	1909
New York	1883	1917
Oregon	1929[5]	1913
Wisconsin	1905	1909

[1] Data obtained from legal sources and verified by correspondence with state governmental and educational officials.
[2] No law, but appointments to District of Columbia government positions are commonly made from the eligible registers of the U. S. Civil Service Commission.
[3] Inoperative since 1922.
[4] Limited in application to inspectors under the dairy and food department.
[5] Applies only to Multonomah County.

of laws save for two exceptions, i.e., Maryland and Oregon. From this it might be deduced that the one type of legislation was instrumental in producing the other.

Comparison of Civil Service and Indefinite Tenure Laws

Although civil service and indefinite teacher tenure have much in common, they also exhibit marked dissimilarities both with respect to origin and fundamental purposes. Federal and state civil service laws and regulations, as they exist to-day, grew out

Development of Legislation

of the thoroughly vicious spoils system and attempt very definitely to establish merit as the sole criterion for entrance into, and promotion and retention in, government employ. To a much smaller degree, as will be shown, indefinite tenure legislation resulted from a protest against political control of the schools and a desire on the part of teachers and board members to institute a merit system for teachers. A brief review of civil service history and of certain features of indefinite tenure history will demonstrate clearly the differences in origin.

The spoils system in the federal civil service came into existence with the Jackson administration in 1829, the new President availing himself of the opportunity afforded by the four-year tenure of office law of 1820 to indulge in wholesale dismissals and new appointments. Conditions gradually grew worse from this time until 1845 when the practice reached its highest point, there to remain until 1865.[2] The extremes to which it was carried is indicated by the complaint of a Washington correspondent of a New York City newspaper, who stated that the spoils system threatened to bring more evils upon the nation than any dozen other elements "conspiring, as it were, to entirely change the character of the Government of the United States."[3] Civil service was defined in the first party platform to advocate reform as

a mere instrument of partisan tyranny and personal ambition, and an object of selfish greed. It is a scandal and a reproach upon free institutions, and breeds a demoralization dangerous to the perpetuity of republican government.[4]

Attempts at reform are recorded as early as 1851 and 1853, but the first serious attempt came in 1865 with the introduction of the Jenckes bill in Congress. Other ineffectual attempts followed and gradually the public became aroused; civil service reform was an issue in several instances in the fall elections of 1882, doubtless owing in part to the death of President Garfield at the hands of a disappointed office-seeker during the previous year. In 1883 the famous Pendleton reform bill, still the basic law of the federal civil service, was passed by Congress. Briefly, this bill established standards for selection of civil employees and purported to remove the service from the field of politics. Some state laws were passed

[2] *A Brief History of the U.S. Civil Service*, p. 12. U.S. Civil Service Commission, 1929.
[3] *Ibid.*, p. 15
[4] *Ibid.*, p. 18.

shortly after this, as Table I shows, and all may be said to have been enacted to combat the evils of the spoils system.

Proof of the existence of a spoils system in the field of education is not so profuse and convincing as in the field of civil service. Supporters of indefinite tenure from the beginning almost down to the present time have claimed that they were fighting a war against politics in education and to some extent their assertions have been true. Personal favoritism and political preference have played important parts in teacher personnel practices, but these influences have never been as strong or the system as reprehensible as was the case with civil service. A typical statement with regard to the spoils system in education appeared in a *Research Bulletin* of the National Education Association in 1924:

> Those who are familiar with the situation believe that one of the gravest dangers that confront the American public school system today is to be found in the attempts of groups of machine politicians, who seek to control and in many cases do control, the local government in our large municipalities. These machine politicians attempt to control the administration of the schools and use them for political purposes. We mean by this for purposes of patronage and spoils.[5]

Of late, as intimated above, such claims have decreased both in intensity and frequency. This decrease in comments on the subject, the absence of any considerable amount of information regarding it, and the added fact that the public has never been aroused all indicate that political dangers have probably been over-emphasized by sponsors of indefinite tenure.

With regard to basic purposes, civil service differs from indefinite tenure in one important particular and is similar in another. A publication of the national government states the major aim of the federal civil service in these words:

> The fundamental purpose of the civil service law was to establish, in the parts of the service covered by its provisions, a merit system whereby selection for appointment should be made upon the basis of demonstrated relative fitness, without regard to political, religious, or other considerations. To carry out this purpose a plan of competitive examinations is prescribed.[6]

Another purpose which, at least in the public mind, is just as important is that of protection of the employee during efficient service. The fundamental mission of indefinite tenure, as will be

---
[5] *N.E.A. Research Bul.*, Vol. 2, No. 5, p. 146, Nov. 1924.

[6] *General Information Regarding the U.S. Civil Service*, p. 1. U.S. Civil Service Commission, 1931.

Development of Legislation

shown in later chapters, is to safeguard teachers in their positions. Indefinite tenure statutes as such, although professedly created to aid in developing a strong and able profession, contain hardly any provisions—indeed, in some cases none at all—aimed at control of entrance into the profession.

Another important difference is that retirement laws are always a corollary of civil service, while they may or may not exist in conjunction with indefinite tenure.

ACTIVITIES AND INFLUENCE OF THE NATIONAL EDUCATION ASSOCIATION

Next to state teachers' associations, the National Education Association has doubtless been the most influential of all professional organizations that have sponsored indefinite tenure legislation. Its interest in making teacher tenure more secure dates back almost one-half century, yet its activities to secure protective legislation have been confined largely to the last thirteen or fourteen years.

The earliest study of tenure by a committee of the Association, as far as the writer could ascertain, was reported at the annual meeting of the Association in 1887.[7] This study pointed out the fact that the teacher was not a member of a profession but a hireling in need of more secure tenure; it recommended exposition of the evils of the then present system, better training for teachers, and increased compensation, predicting that agitation of these subjects would lead to legislation. No other early report on tenure was found by the writer. In 1905 a committee bearing the title "Committee Upon Salaries, Tenure of Office, and Pension Provisions of Teachers" rendered a report in which tenure was dismissed with the terse comment that sufficient material (evidently statistical) was available in the United States Bureau of Education.[8] Open advocacy by the Association of safeguarded tenure appears as early as 1915[9] and the following year the first definite recommendation of protective legislation appears in the records.[10] During these years security of tenure was considered along with adequate salaries and suitable retirement allowances,

[7] *N.E.A. Addresses and Proc.*, 1887, pp. 307-11.
[8] *N.E.A. Report on Salaries, Tenure, and Pensions in the U. S.*, July 1905, p. 151.
[9] *N.E.A. Addresses and Proc.*, 1915, Vol. 53, p. 29.
[10] *N.E.A. Addresses and Proc.*, 1916, Vol. 54, p. 27.

the assumption being that realization of these goals would, through improving the teacher's status, naturally improve the excellence of the public schools.

In 1911 the Association appointed a committee which during the greater part of its eleven- or twelve-year existence was known as the "Committee on Teachers' Salaries, Tenure, and Pensions" and which during the first nine years of its life concentrated attention on salaries and retirement. This committee presented a preliminary report on tenure to the Association in 1920, stating that it wished to do for tenure what had already been done for salaries and pensions.[11] Specialization of function within the Committee appeared the following year, the report for 1921 showing the Committee divided into three subdivisions with a chairman in charge of each. The four reports issued by the Subcommittee on tenure are as follows: 1920, general survey of conditions and proposal of questions for study; 1921, history of tenure, need for it, and discussion of fundamental provisions of a law; 1922, digest of laws then in force, discussion of California tenure law, and a copy of the proposed Ohio law; 1923, existing tenure laws, pending measures, principles underlying indefinite teacher tenure laws, and the experience of California with its law. A tabular condensation of the digest of laws in the 1922 report was included, along with certain additional material on the subject, in a 1923 issue of the *Research Bulletin* of the Association,[12] which touched on six phases of education and was issued "with the sessions of the State Legislatures in mind."

With the appointment of the Tenure Committee of One Hundred in 1923, which Committee still functions to-day, began the most aggressive period in the history of the Association's support of indefinite tenure. The most energetic chairman this Committee has had once defined the work of the Committee as that of surveying prevailing tendencies and legislative provisions for the tenure of teachers in the school systems of the several states and making available the salient facts for all interested in the problem.[13] In the year following its creation, the Committee issued its most ambitious and perhaps its best report. Since this report was reviewed in Chapter I (pages 4-5), it will be dismissed

[11] *N.E.A. Addresses and Proc.*, 1920, Vol. 58, p. 148.
[12] *N.E.A. Research Bul.*, Vol. 1, No. 1, pp. 54-57, Jan. 1923.
[13] Hunter, Fred M., Report of the Tenure Committee . . . , *N.E.A. Addresses and Proc.*, 1928, Vol. 66, p. 204.

Development of Legislation

here with the statement that its chief value lies in its presentation of current conditions and of mass professional opinion concerning causes for dismissal.

The more important contents of other reports of the Committee have been as follows: 1925, report of an investigation of tenure in colleges and normal schools; 1926, teacher turnover and an extended bibliography on teacher tenure; 1927, tentative statement of principles for the framing and operation of indefinite tenure laws, further data on turnover, information regarding recruits in the profession, and three newly enacted laws; 1928, review of previous reports and restatement of principles, and cursory studies of the operation of the Massachusetts and New Jersey laws; 1929, no report; 1930, report of further study along established lines and advocation of a series of intensive studies in typical areas, similar to the Holmstedt study of the New Jersey law (page 5), then in progress; 1931, abstract of the Holmstedt study; 1932, survey of the legal conditions of tenure in the forty-eight states.

The reports of the Committee of One Hundred mirror an interesting and noteworthy change in the attitude of the Association toward indefinite tenure. From 1924 to 1928, inclusive, the fervor of the Association for the movement tended to outrun its reason, as is shown by the following relatively unsupported statement appearing in one report:

> The teachers of the community must carry the case for tenure to the public as a movement in behalf of the schools and the children. To back them in this, they have indisputable evidence showing that indefinite tenure works in the interest of a more permanent and abler teaching body, and that more competent young people are thereby attracted to the profession.[14]

"Indisputable evidence" collected by all committees of the Association prior to the issuance of this statement represented largely the outcomes of a priori reasoning, analytical studies of the provisions of indefinite tenure laws, cursory studies of their operation, and surveys of professional opinion. Until 1928, the Association used every means at its disposal to popularize and further the cause of protective tenure; but since then its activities in this regard have waned decidedly. Recent reports of the Committee have been brief and free from expressions of opinion.

Some idea of the influence of the Association on the indefinite

[14] *N.E.A. Addresses and Proc.*, 1926, Vol. 64, p. 204.

tenure movement may be obtained from a statement appearing in the Committee's report for 1928:

> Thousands of copies of these reports have been available to members of the teaching profession, to laymen, to committees of legislatures, and to others interested in the problems of the profession. The data assembled by the work of the members of this Committee have had influence in determining the attitude of teacher organizations and of legislatures in arriving at sound judgment of tenure policies.[15]

The 1924 report particularly was said to have received wide circulation and to have been used in state and local campaigns for teacher tenure legislation.[16] From 1920, when the Association began its active campaign for protected tenure, until the present time, a number of state legislatures have considered indefinite tenure bills and five have enacted such bills into law. It should be noted, however, that three of these were passed early in the period, namely, in 1921 and 1922. Two other states have passed continuing contract laws since 1920, i.e., Pennsylvania and Nevada. An indefinite tenure bill was introduced in the 1925 Pennsylvania legislature which was reported to be the result of a study made by a state committee in coöperation with the National Education Association Committee of One Hundred,[17] but this failed of passage.

The often expressed purpose of the Association in promoting protective tenure is laudable enough. It has claimed to see in the device the best method of furthering the development of a sound and stable teaching profession, compatible with the educational interests of society, the needs of children, and fairness to teachers.[18] To some extent its position has, of course, been tenable; but its over-zealousness for a number of years has doubtless caused many members of the profession to regard a considerable proportion of its reports on indefinite tenure as a mixture of fact and propaganda, with the latter predominating.

THE AMERICAN FEDERATION OF TEACHERS AND INDEFINITE TENURE

In its characteristically militant manner, the American Federation of Teachers has stood for protective teacher tenure since its

---
[15] N.E.A. Addresses and Proc., 1928, Vol. 66, p. 205.
[16] Footnote Ref. No. 14, p. 205.
[17] "Tenure Bill," Pa. State Jl., Vol. 73, No. 6, p. 351, Feb. 1925.
[18] N.E.A. Addresses and Proc., 1927, Vol. 65, p. 209.

Development of Legislation

organization in 1916. During much or all of this time, it has maintained a permanent committee on tenure and has attempted through this body, through its state and local organizations, and by means of its official organ, the *American Teacher*, to bring about the enactment of protective laws. The Federation not only claims that its local units are among the first professional organizations to advocate guaranteed tenure for teachers and to secure sound laws, but that the American Federation of Labor, of which it is an integral part, is the only group of non-teaching organized citizenry in America on record for teacher tenure based on efficiency.[19] Reasons given by the Federation for its ardent espousal of indefinite tenure are that such protection will give a professional standing, will attract high grade people to public school work, and that the increased freedom accruing from it will give us better schools and a better nation.

It may be claimed that the Federation is partly responsible for the existence of several state laws, since it is relatively strong in a number of states where statutes have been enacted. The local units in California and also the state organization there are reported to have coöperated in the passage of the 1921 law;[20] while the local units of Chicago claim credit for the Illinois law.[21]

> One of the first tenure laws ever passed in the United States was the Chicago law, secured by Locals 1, 2, and 3 of the American Federation of Teachers with the backing and assistance of Organized Labor in the face of the opposition of the Association of Commerce, Civic Federation, and similar groups.[21]

RÔLE OF STATE TEACHERS' ASSOCIATIONS

Both in states that now have indefinite teacher tenure laws and in a number where unsuccessful campaigns have been waged, state teachers' associations have been active in promoting the cause of protected service. Clear proof of such activity in California, Indiana, Massachusetts, and New Jersey appears in the official publications of the associations of these states. Information received directly from the executive secretaries of state associations add three other states to the list, namely, Louisiana, Minnesota, and

---

[19] "Teacher Tenure," p. 1. Paper prepared by F. C. Hanson for use in the Pa. Campaign. In Ms. (1931).
[20] Minard, Jeanette, "California Tenure Law," *Am. Teacher*, No. 8, Vol. 12, pp. 4-5, April 1928.
[21] Footnote Ref. No. 19, p. 8.

New York; and evidence from Alexander's study[22] corroborates the reports for New Jersey and New York, while adding Colorado to the list.

Alexander (*supra*[22]) points out that although "permanent tenure of office has long been set up as an ideal by the associations," it was only shortly before the publication of his report (in 1910) that they began working very definitely for it. According to this authority, the New York Association began activities at least as early as 1904; the Colorado Association initiated consideration of such legislation in 1907; and the New Jersey Association began its campaign in 1903. Alexander credited the New Jersey Association with being the most aggressive of all those that had promoted indefinite tenure before 1910, stating that after adoption of the principle in 1903, successive legislative committees had from 1905 on gradually broken down opposition on the part of legislators and the public, as well as different beliefs concerning the matter on the part of teachers, and had achieved passage of a law in 1909.

Granrud[23] states that a large number of teachers' associations have probably had considerable influence in the passage of educational legislation, but does not mention indefinite tenure laws specifically. Where associations have sponsored protective tenure campaigns, promotive activities have commonly been in the hands of special or standing tenure committees, which have customarily worked in conjunction with committees on legislation.

The California Teachers' Association has probably been the most active in the country in promoting education legislation in general and deserves much credit for the passage and maintenance of indefinite tenure laws in the state. A bill presented by the Association in 1919 was defeated; but a bill framed along the same lines, although not originated by the Association, was enacted into law in 1921.[24] Since that time the organization has had to defend the law against numerous enemies; it reported in 1923 that one of the bitterest conflicts of the legislative session raged around the Dozier bill, which attempted to do away with tenure

---

[22] Alexander, Carter, *The Work of Teachers' Voluntary Associations*, pp. 52-53.
[23] Granrud, John, *The Organization and Objectives of State Teachers' Associations*, p. 43.
[24] "School Legislation," *Sierra Ed. News*, Vol. 17, No. 4, pp. 185-86, April 1921; "Educational Measures Now before the Governor," *Sierra Ed. News*, Vol. 17, No. 6, pp. 310-11, Jan. 1921.

Development of Legislation

protection,[25] and that no lengthy new program had been undertaken since it seemed more expedient to hold determinedly the gains of two years previous, advances that embraced considerably more than protective tenure.[26] In 1925 the Association attempted unsuccessfully to secure the enactment of a new law, the original being considered discriminatory; two years later a bill that the Association supported was passed by the state legislature.[27] Again in 1931 the Association presented a new bill, which, after being amended, was made law.[28]

Soon after the Indiana law was passed in 1927, the state superintendent of public instruction made the following statement in a public address on tenure:

> The Indiana State Teachers' Association has consistently advocated the adoption of this measure as one of the steps necessary for the development of a real profession of teaching in our state.[29]

That the state teachers' body is largely responsible for the existence of the indefinite tenure law is evident from an editorial comment which appeared in the *Indiana Teacher* shortly after the statute was enacted:

> In 1926 the state association, at its annual meeting, passed a resolution in favor of a tenure law. It therefore became the duty of the legislative committee to frame a tenure bill and use its best efforts to secure its passage. As there was no further instruction to this committee, its program consisted of the passage of the tenure bill and the protection of the schools from the passage of adverse legislation.[30]

During the legislative session of 1929, a strong effort was made by foes of indefinite tenure to repeal the state law, but this move was reported as having been thwarted by the teaching profession through its several organizations, of which the Indiana State Teachers' Association is the most important.[31]

Statements that have appeared from time to time in the official

---

[25] Keppel, Mark, "School Legislation in 1923," *Sierra Ed. News*, Vol. 19, No. 7, p. 414, Sept. 1923.
[26] "The Legislative Situation" (Ed.), *Sierra Ed. News*, Vol. 19, No. 6, p. 310, Jan. 1923.
[27] Carr, W. G., "Teacher Tenure in California," *Sierra Ed. News*, Vol. 24, No. 7, p. 23, Sept. 1928.
[28] Cloud, Roy W., "The Legislature: Finale," *Sierra Ed. News*, Vol. 27, No. 7, p. 13, Sept. 1931.
[29] Wisehart, Roy P., "Some Phases of Teacher Tenure in Indiana," *Ind. Univ. Bul.*, Vol. 4, No. 4, pp. 45-48, March 1928.
[30] "The Legislative Program" (Ed.), *Ind. Teacher*, Vol. 73, No. 3, p. 16, Nov. 1928.
[31] "Victory for Tenure" (Ed.), *Ind. Teacher*, Vol. 73, No. 8, pp. 16-17, April 1929.

organ of the Massachusetts Teachers' Federation (a state association), under the head of "The Service of the Federation to the Teachers of Massachusetts," indicate that the Federation considers the indefinite tenure law one of its achievements. An editorial in the official magazine gives this review of the early history of the law:

> Consideration of the subject of tenure is of comparatively recent date. In 1913 the Federation took up this matter in connection with pension legislation. . . .
> The bill introduced in 1913 was modeled upon the New Jersey law. The Committee on Education at first refused to report the bill, but our friends in the House induced the committee to change its mind. The Bill passed the House, the Senate, was vetoed by the Governor, passed the House over the Governor's veto, and was lost in the Senate.
> The activity and success of the Federation in promoting the subject of tenure in 1913 had aroused the interest of the State Board of Education, and its bill "Relative to the Tenure of Office of Teachers and Superintendents of Public Schools" became law June 29, 1914. . . .[32]

The Federation has also been active in bringing about at least one of the two amendments to the law.[33]

Some of the general activities and influence of the New Jersey State Teachers' Association with regard to indefinite tenure have already been noted (page 18). Alexander states that in 1908, during the campaign for the tenure-of-office bill, the Association sent out 10,000 circulars to be used as campaign documents and quotes from the report of the legislative committee for 1908 as follows:

> Immediately after the organization, in January, the committee rallied all the forces it could reach in the effort to secure the passage of the bill. Every member of the Senate and Assembly was interviewed by members of the committee or by other advocates of the bill.
> . . . A number of the leading city superintendents of the state came with the members of the committee and the president of the association to present the claims of the bill at the preliminary hearing in the committees of the Senate and made addresses in its behalf at the public hearing in the Assembly. Large delegations of teachers from different parts of the state attended the hearing.[34]

The Minnesota law, although supported by the State Teachers' Association, was promoted mainly by teachers in the three cities to

---

[32] "Tenure" (Ed.), *Common Ground*, Vol. 1, No. 13, pp. 16-17, April 1920.
[33] "Legislative Matters," *Common Ground*, Vol. 2, No. 3, p. 49, July 1921.
[34] Alexander, *op. cit.*, pp. 33-34.

Development of Legislation

which it applies, viz.: Duluth, Minneapolis, and Saint Paul.[35] As for the other state laws, no evidence save that already cited (page 17f.) was found showing the extent to which they owe their creation to the teachers' associations in the respective states.

No valid criticism can be made of the reasons state teachers' associations have given for supporting indefinite tenure laws. The most common ones are: (1) provision of security for teachers; (2) development of a true teaching profession; (3) increase in efficiency and competency of teachers; and (4) protection of the interests of children (or of the schools, or of both). In the main, the claims set forth have been the same as those made by the National Education Association. The protection feature has apparently appealed to state associations more than any other and they seem to have accepted almost without question the supposition that protection in and of itself would produce the other desirable ends. A quotation or two from articles on tenure in association journals will show the general nature of the claims that have been made.

The *Indiana Teacher* contributes the following emphatic expression of the protection idea, which, however, was quoted by the aforementioned magazine from a state newspaper:

> To those who espoused the measure and fought long and hard for its enactment it stands as a writ of emancipation from their enslavement to politics and the whims of superior authorities. Teachers who had been forced to cringe before the lash of domineering trustees, superintendents and principals hailed the Legislature's act as a guarantee of individual self-respect and the opportunity of devoting their best thoughts toward the education of children and not toward catering to the powers in whose hands their destinies rested.[36]

Practically all of the claims listed above are embodied in this statement from the *Sierra Educational News,* of California:

> It must be thoroughly understood that tenure, important as it may be to the teachers involved, is primarily needed in the interest of the schools and the children. Proper tenure lends itself to improving the stability of the profession. A thoroughly adequate tenure law does not protect the incompetent teacher, as many suppose. It protects the community against the incompetent teacher and through promise of added stability, secures and holds in the profession, those men and women best qualified to teach.[37]

---

[35] Letter from C. G. Schulz, Sec. Minn. State Teachers' Ass'n, under date Oct. 1931.
[36] "The Teacher Tenure Law" (Ed.), Quoted from the *Anderson Herald* in the *Ind. Teacher*, Vol. 76, No. 4, p. 15, Dec. 1931.
[37] Chamberlain, Henry Arthur, "The Legislative Outlook," *Sierra Ed. News*, Vol. 22, No. 6, pp. 379-80, June 1926.

CHRONOLOGICAL REVIEW OF INDEFINITE TENURE LEGISLATION

Chronological facts for indefinite tenure laws taken alone indicate that such laws have come into being in some states only after repeated attempts to secure their passage and have been retained on the statute books at the expense of vigilant effort on the part of supporters, while in other states initial passage was not difficult and retention has not been a problem. A review of actual dates of passage of the several state laws, with dates of immediately preceding strong attempts to secure passage in some cases, and subsequent repeal and amendment attempts regardless of their outcome, will reveal the significance of this statement.

The District of Columbia appears to have been the first governmental unit in the United States with rank higher than that of an ordinary city, to grant teachers continuous tenure during efficient service and good behavior. Board rules of 1906 or 1907, based on the organic act of 1906 or created under authority of this act, specifically guarantee teachers protected tenure.[38] To-day board rules are evidently as important where indefinite tenure is concerned as the education law, there being no division of the law given over to the subject. One District school official with whom the writer had a conference stated that provision of protective tenure is "steeped in practice and precedent."

As was stated in another connection (page 18), indefinite tenure was agitated in New Jersey from 1903 to 1909, when an effective law was secured. This law stands to-day in exactly the same form in which it was enacted, despite a dozen or more attempts to repeal or amend it. Holmstedt,[39] mentions four efforts to increase the length of the probationary period and seven different repeal attempts, the last in 1925 after the law had been in operation sixteen years. An effort was made by the 1932 legislature to repeal the mandatory salary clause of the law, but this failed.

Oregon enacted its indefinite tenure law in 1913 and amended it in 1917 and 1921. Agitation for a law in Massachusetts began in 1913 and the present law was passed the next year (*supra*[32]). It was amended in 1918 and 1921. Several other attempts to

---

[38] Rules for the Governing of the Public Schools of the District of Columbia, 1907, Sec. 20.

[39] Holmstedt, Raleigh W., *A Study of the Effects of the Teacher Tenure Law in New Jersey*, pp. 83-84.

Development of Legislation 23

amend the law so as to have it provide for appeal by dismissed teachers to the Commissioner of Education and to include a list of acceptable reasons for the dismissal of teachers have been fruitless.[40]

It appears probable that the three largest cities of New York, i.e., Buffalo, New York City, and Rochester, had indefinite tenure either under board rules or special legislation prior to the passage of the law now operative in 1917; but concrete proof of this was not found. The present law has been amended once for the purpose of extending protection to certain non-educational school employees.[41]

Maryland legislated its indefinite tenure provisions in 1916[42] and added to them in 1927 the requirement that teachers be members of the state teachers' retirement system. The Illinois law was passed in 1917[43] and has not been amended. Wisconsin passed its law in 1909[44] and in 1925 reduced its probationary requirement from four to three years.[45]

The California law has had a checkered and interesting history, rivaling all others for variety. In 1911 the state legislature passed the first tenure regulations for public schools, these providing mainly for automatic reëlection of teachers unless notified contrariwise by or before the tenth of June.[46] An indefinite tenure bill proposed in 1919 failed, but a similar bill was made law in 1921. In 1923 a determined but unsuccessful attempt to repeal the bill was made (*supra*[25]). An attempt at amendment which amounted to complete revision failed in 1925, but a new law was enacted in 1927; also in 1931 a complete new law was put on the statute books.

Colorado and Louisiana passed their laws in 1921 and 1922, respectively. The Indiana law came into existence in 1927 and vigorous attempts to repeal it were made in 1929 and 1931. The Minnesota law also was a product of 1927.

Indefinite tenure laws have either gone into effect immediately upon enactment or shortly thereafter.

[40] Letter from Hugh Nixon, Sec. Mass. Teachers' Fed., under date Oct. 14, 1931.
[41] Education Law, 1932, Chap. 594, Par. 872, Subd. 2-a, Law 1923, p. 260.
[42] Laws of the State of Maryland, 1916, Chap. 506, Sec. 25J, p. 1012.
[43] Revised Statutes of the State of Illinois, 1931, pp. 2529-530, 2536.
[44] Laws of Wisconsin, 1909, Chap. 510, Sec. 17, pp. 658-59.
[45] Nyberg *v.* Milwaukee et al., 209 N. W. 683 (1926).
[46] Cloud, Roy W., "In re Tenure" (Preprint), *Sierra Ed. News*, Jan. 1931.

SUMMARY

Indefinite teacher tenure apparently owes its existence largely to the civil service and to the activities of professional organizations, the most important of which are the National Education Association, the American Federation of Teachers, and state teachers' associations. The public, generally speaking, has been apathetic toward the matter; as far as the writer could learn, only one non-professional organization, i.e., the American Federation of Labor, is on record as favoring it. Professional organizations have been interested mainly in providing protection for teachers, although they have professed as great or greater desire to safeguard the interests of the school and of children. They commonly have proceeded on the supposition that the former would *ipso facto* produce the latter. Summary facts concerning the separate major developmental forces follow.

1. Indefinite teacher tenure is a modified application of the civil service principle and its legal development has been considerably influenced by civil service laws and practices. Ten of the twelve states that have either general or restricted civil service laws also have indefinite tenure laws, and, more important, the former antedated the latter in all but two cases. Federal and state civil service laws owe their origin to the spoils system, which grew so objectionable that the public became interested in reform. Indefinite tenure laws have been enacted partly to rid teacher personnel practices of the evils of political influence, but the menace has never been as great in the public schools as in other fields of governmental service. The fundamental purpose of civil service has been to establish merit as the basis for service; whereas indefinite tenure, although professing to be a merit system, has neglected this principle. Protection is a secondary aim of civil service and the major goal of indefinite tenure.

2. The National Education Association has advocated protective tenure for almost a half-century, but its promotive activities have been confined largely to the last thirteen or fourteen years. It has carried on its work principally through committees and since 1923 has had a committee (Tenure Committee of One Hundred) whose duty it has been to study the problem, prepare reports, and exert its influence to produce legislation. Reports of this Commit-

Development of Legislation

tee have been widely circulated. All of them have contained valuable material, but, on the whole, they have savored too much of propaganda. In fairness to the Association, however, it should be noted that recent reports have been unbiased and that the Association has been much less aggressive in its support of safeguarded tenure than it was from, say, 1921 to 1928, inclusive.

3. The American Federation of Teachers has sponsored indefinite tenure in its habitually militant manner since its organization in 1916. It claims full credit for the Illinois law and partial credit for the California one. There is reason to believe that it has had influence elsewhere.

4. State teachers' associations have beyond a doubt been the most influential of the forces making for protective tenure. This study presents proof that eight of the twelve state laws owe their existence in some degree to state associations. In some states associations have left no stones unturned in their promotive and defensive efforts, while in others they have done much less than they might have.

5. Evidence adduced in this chapter, including the chronological review, indicates that passage of laws has been attained in some states by dint of great effort and retained by constant vigilance, whereas neither passage nor retention has been difficult in others.

SELECTED REFERENCES

ALEXANDER, CARTER. *The Work of Teachers' Voluntary Associations.* Bureau of Publications, Teachers College, Columbia University, New York, 1910.

AMERICAN FEDERATION OF TEACHERS. "Teacher Tenure: Report of the Permanent Committee to the American Federation of Teachers, 1929 Convention." *American Teacher,* 14:20-23, December 1929.

CLOUD, ROY W. "In re Tenure." (Preprint.) *Sierra Educational News,* January 1931.

CORPSTEIN, SUSIE and DUPUY, E. J. "Retrospection." *American Teacher,* 15:2, May 1931.

GRANRUD, JOHN. *The Organization and Objectives of State Teachers' Associations.* Contributions to Education, No. 234. Bureau of Publications, Teachers College, Columbia University, New York, 1926.

MARSH, EDWARD CLARK. *The Civil Service.* National Civil Service Reform League, New York, 1922.

MINARD, JEANNETTE. "California Tenure Law." *American Teacher,* 12:4-5, April 1928.

NATIONAL CIVIL SERVICE REFORM LEAGUE. *The Story of the Merit System in the Civil Service.* New York, 1929.
NATIONAL EDUCATION ASSOCIATION. *Addresses and Proceedings,* 1885-1932.
UNITED STATES CIVIL SERVICE COMMISSION. *A Brief History of the United States Civil Service.* Washington, D. C., 1929.
UNITED STATES CIVIL SERVICE COMMISSION. *Civil Service Act and Rules—Statutes, Executive Orders and Regulations.* Washington, D. C., 1930.
UNITED STATES CIVIL SERVICE COMMISSION. *General Information Regarding the United States Civil Service.* Washington, D. C., 1932.

CHAPTER III

Analysis and Evaluation According to Established Criteria of Existing Indefinite Tenure Laws

ANALYSIS

To AID in making clear the existing protective tenure situation, this section presents an analysis of laws in force as of June, 1932.

The tables presented are based not only on the laws themselves, but also on interpretations and supplementary facts received from the several state departments of education represented and on sections of the respective education laws closely related to the tenure sections. In the six tables there are twenty-three items of information received directly from state departments and fourteen taken from related provisions of the education laws, all of each type being clearly designated. This procedure was necessary, if a complete picture was to be given, since the separate laws are all vague in some respects and incomplete in others. The finished analysis shows several of the laws markedly deficient in a number of apparently important matters; witness the fifty-five blank spaces in Tables II to VII, inclusive.

According to Table II, only two states, Indiana and New Jersey, have state-wide indefinite tenure laws; two others, Massachusetts and Maryland, have laws which apply in all districts except the largest city of each state; and the California law is state-wide in principle but optional in its application to small districts. The laws of six states apply only to large cities therein, and the District of Columbia law makes a seventh of this type; while the New York law applies to all cities of the state. Employees protected ordinarily include all educational workers concerned directly with classroom instruction, i.e., teachers, supervisors, principals. Higher administrative officers, i.e., superintendents and assistants, are not as a rule included, the exceptions being as follows: the California law protects superintendents, as well as other

TABLE II

APPLICATION OF INDEFINITE TEACHER TENURE LAWS, EDUCATIONAL QUALIFICATIONS FOR PROTECTION THEREUNDER, AND PROBATIONARY PERIODS PROVIDED[1]

State	Application — To Districts	Application — To School Employees	Educational Requirements	Probationary Period[2]
California	All districts with 850 A.D.A. or above; optional with those below.	Every certificated employee; administrators and supervisors are classified as classroom teachers unless local regulations provide otherwise.	Certificate of type required for position held.	Three school years. Longer periods optional in districts having less than 850 A.D.A.; 75% attendance during a school year gives full credit.
Colorado	Districts of first class having 20,000 or more inhabitants: Denver, Colorado Springs, and Pueblo.	All teachers.	Certificate required by state law.[3]	Three years.
District of Columbia	Entire district.†	Teachers, school officers, and other educational employees; superintendents not included.	Board of examiners' certificate.[4]	One year.
Illinois	Cities of 500,000 or more: Chicago.	All members of the teaching force, except the superintendent, assistant and district superintendents, and members of the board of examiners.	Board of examiners' certificate.	Three years.
Indiana	All school units.	Licensed teachers, supervisors, and principals in all school corporations; and licensed assistant superintendents and superintendents in school cities and towns.	State license.	Five years.
Louisiana	Orleans Parish: the City of New Orleans.	All properly certificated teachers.	Proper state certificates.	Three years.

Analysis and Evaluation of Tenure Laws

TABLE II—Continued

State	Application To Districts	Application To School Employees	Educational Requirements	Probationary Period[2]
Maryland	All counties (*i.e.*, school units), Baltimore City excepted.	All teachers and principals.	Certificate required by state law.[3]	Two years.
Massachusetts	All of state except Boston.	Teachers and superintendents, except union or district superintendents.—†In reality, no superintendents have indefinite tenure.	Certificate required locally or by state law in the case of state-aided high schools.†	Three years, with option of period as short as one year at discretion of local school committee.
Minnesota	First class cities: Duluth, Minneapolis, and St. Paul.	All educational employees concerned directly with classroom instruction.	Certificate required by state law.[3]	Three years.
New Jersey	All districts.	Teachers, principals, and supervising principals.	Proper state teacher's certificate.	Three years, unless shorter period is fixed by employing board.
New York	All cities of the state.[5]	All members of the teaching and supervising staff, except associate superintendents and examiners.	Requirements of law and the State Department.	One to three years, at discretion of local board.
Oregon	All school districts with population of 20,000 or more: Portland and Salem.	All supervisors, principals, vice principals, and instructors.	Certificate required by state law.[3]	Two years.
Wisconsin	First class cities: Milwaukee.	All members of the teaching and supervisory force except the superintendent, assistant superintendents, and special supervisors.	Certificate required by state law.[3]	Three years.

[1] Information obtained from latest editions of the respective school codes.
[2] Periods given represent consecutive school years.
[3] Requirement appears only in the certification section of the school code.
[4] Compilation of Laws Affecting the Public Schools, 1804-1929, District of Columbia, p. 21.
[5] Article 33-A, pp. 248 ff., of the Education Law, 1931.
† Interpretation or information was received from state department.

TABLE III

SUSPENSION AND DISMISSAL PROVISIONS OF INDEFINITE TENURE LAWS FOR DISCIPLINE OF PERMANENT TEACHERS[1]

State	Suspension	Dismissal
California	Immediate suspension for charges of immoral conduct, which becomes complete dismissal if teacher fails to demand hearing within thirty days.—†Temporary suspension may also be used as disciplinary measure after charges against a teacher are proven.	Dismissal by governing board. Effective at end of school year for all causes except immoral conduct, unless teacher demands hearing.
Colorado		Board of directors dismisses after serving charges and holding a hearing. Summary dismissal possible by two-thirds or greater vote of board when recommended by district superintendent and the principal or other supervisor.
District of Columbia	Suspension for violation of board rules, absence without leave, disobedience or neglect of orders, other offences against morality and good order, and incompetency. Unless otherwise specified, suspension extends only until the next meeting of the board.—†Temporary suspension may be inflicted by the board as a disciplinary measure.	Board dismisses upon written recommendation of superintendent of schools, in accordance with rules and statutes. Hearing granted if desired.
Illinois	Suspension as prescribed by board rules pending hearing of charges.	Board dismisses by majority vote after hearing, upon written charges presented by the superintendent.
Indiana	Any teacher may be suspended pending cancellation of contract proceedings.	School board of any city or town, by majority vote, or a township trustee may cancel an indefinite contract after complying with provisions of the law.
Louisiana		Board dismisses (following investigation and report) when it finds teacher guilty of any charge for which dismissal is the penalty.—[2]Teacher given opportunity for a hearing.

TABLE III—*Continued*

State	Suspension	Dismissal
Maryland	County board suspends upon recommendation of county superintendent after giving teacher opportunity to be heard; grounds same as for dismissal.	Same as suspension provision.
Massachusetts	School committee may suspend either teacher or superintendent for unbecoming conduct.	School committee dismisses by two-thirds vote of entire membership, after giving teacher opportunity for a hearing. Recommendation of superintendent necessary for dismissal of a teacher.
Minnesota	School board or commissioner may suspend teacher upon filing of charges, and as a disciplinary measure after hearing.	School board by majority vote, or a school commissioner may dismiss a teacher after according her a hearing.
New Jersey	Superintendent, with approval of president of board, may suspend assistant superintendent, principal, or teacher. Must report action to board which takes action to restore or remove.[3]	Dismissal after hearing, by majority vote of board.
New York		Board of education dismisses after hearing, by majority vote.
Oregon	Board may summarily suspend teacher for gross dereliction of duty or for misconduct. This amounts to dismissal if teacher does not ask for hearing.	Board dismisses after hearing. Action final if five members of board concur in the action.
Wisconsin		Board dismisses, after investigation and hearing if requested by the teacher.

[1] Information obtained from latest editions of the respective school codes.
[2] Public School Laws of Louisiana, 1926, Sec. 48, p. 171.
[3] Article VI, Sec. 105 (69), p. 46, New Jersey School Laws, 1931.
† Interpretation or information was received from state department.

administrative and supervisory officers, on the same basis as classroom teachers; superintendents in school cities and towns of Indiana are eligible for permanent status; and the Massachusetts law extends protection to certain types of superintendents, although this provision does not hold in practice.

Table II further shows that only six indefinite tenure laws as such mention in any way educational requirements for teaching. Of course, legal requirements, applying to all public schools, exist in every state except Massachusetts;[1] but the fact that no reference is made to them in seven protective tenure statutes can be interpreted only as a serious deficiency. Three years is the most common probationary requirement, as shown by the same table; nine laws list this number—five without any alternatives, three with provision for shorter periods, and one with provision for a longer period in certain districts. Two years is specified by two laws and one and five by one each.

Suspension and dismissal provisions of the several laws are presented in Table III. Temporary suspension is provided by nine laws, usually pending trial of teachers on charges; but in three states, California, Maryland, and Minnesota, and in the District of Columbia, it apparently may be used as a disciplinary measure. Mandatory hearings are provided by six laws and optional ones by the other seven. In every case the board is the dismissing authority.

Table IV shows legal provisions concerning causes for dismissal, charges, and hearings. Detailed causes are specified in eight laws; in two others, certain causes are implied; a single cause is stipulated by one law, the general nature of causes by another, and the final one states that dismissal shall be for "cause." Written charges are required by ten laws; ordinarily, any interested party may prefer charges, but it is usually assumed that this will be done through the superintendent of schools. A service of notice provision is included in eleven laws; such a provision usually states the number of days before the board action will be taken on a proposed dismissal and may also outline the form of the notice. Ten laws establish the local board as the tribunal before which hearings will be held and another law provides an option of a board committee; provision for use of counsel is made by ten laws and for witnesses by eleven. Details concerning the form of hearings are not usually prescribed; however, the assumption is that they will be held with due diligence and in an orderly manner.

---

[1] Legal requirements for certification in Massachusetts apply only to state-aided high schools; but there are relatively few such institutions (the number was about forty in 1926).

Analysis and Evaluation of Tenure Laws

TABLE IV

CAUSES FOR DISMISSAL, MANNER OF PREFERRING CHARGES, AND NATURE OF HEARING PROVIDED IN INDEFINITE TENURE LAWS[1]

State	Causes of Dismissal	Manner in Which Charges Are Preferred	Notice	Nature of Hearing
California	Immoral or unprofessional conduct, dishonesty, incompetency, evident unfitness for service, persistent violation of or refusal to obey state school laws or reasonable regulations prescribed for the government of public schools. Also, decrease in number of pupils or discontinuance of a particular kind of service.	Written, duly signed, and verified by the person filing them.	Written, sent by registered mail with copy of charges and of Article II of Tenure Law enclosed.	Hearing before board, conducted with due diligence according to rules and regulations fixed by board. Accused employee, the board, and the person who preferred the charges may use counsel and witnesses.
Colorado	Cause not political or religious; object is promotion of efficiency of service.	Charge in writing, signed by person making same, filed with secretary of employing board.	Charge served upon accused for at least thirty days.	Before board. Teacher and person making complaint must be heard, with or without counsel. Testimony must be given orally by witness under oath or affirmation.
District of Columbia	Violation of board rules, disobedience or neglect of orders, other offenses against morality or good order, and incompetency.	In writing, signed by persons making complaint and countersigned by superintendent of schools.	Copy of charges and order to appear before board for trial or investigation.	Before board. For defense, teacher has right to counsel and one friend of own selection; may call any employee of school system as a witness.— †Board, likewise, may have witnesses.
Illinois	For cause.	Written charges presented by the superintendent of	Thirty days.	By board or duly authorized committee of the same. Hearing public upon request of any party.

TABLE IV—*Continued*

State	Causes of Dismissal	Manner in Which Charges Are Preferred	Notice	Nature of Hearing
		schools to the board.—†Any person in Chicago may present charges to the superintendent.		Defendant,—† and also the board, privileged to have counsel. Witnesses may be used.
Indiana	Incompetency, insubordination, neglect of duty, immorality, justifiable decrease in the number of teaching positions, or other good and just cause; but not for political or personal reasons.		In writing; exact date, time, and place of hearing being given. Sent not less than thirty or more than forty days prior to date set.	Before board in cities and towns, and before township trustee in townships. Teacher has right to full statement of reasons for proposed cancellation, to be heard, and to present testimony of witnesses and other evidence.—† Counsel may be used by both parties.
Louisiana	Immorality, neglect of duty, incompetency, malfeasance or non-feasance.	Written: preferred by Orleans Parish Board.		
Maryland	Immorality, misconduct in office, incompetency or wilful neglect of duty.	Charges in writing made by county superintendent to county board.	Not less than ten days' notice.	Before board,—† each party being privileged to have witnesses.
Massachusetts	Decrease in number of pupils.		At least thirty days' notice (of the vote on dismissal).	Before school committee, if hearing is requested, one witness being allowed the accused.
Minnesota	Immoral character, conduct unbecoming of a teacher or insubordination; non-feasance;	In writing, signed by person making same. Any	Ten days' notice, served personally or by reg-	Before school board or commissioner. Witnesses and counsel available to either or both parties.

Analysis and Evaluation of Tenure Laws

TABLE IV—*Concluded*

State	Causes of Dismissal	Manner in Which Charges are Preferred	Notice	Nature of Hearing
	inefficiency; affliction with communicable disease; decrease in number of pupils.	interested person may prefer charges.	istered mail.	Public or private as desired by teacher.
New Jersey	Inefficiency, incapacity, conduct unbecoming of a teacher, other just cause, and decrease in number of pupils.	Written, and signed by person making same.	Reasonable notice.	Before board. Witnesses may be subpœnaed by board for either party; teacher may have counsel,— †and likewise the board.
New York	For cause: inefficiency, incompetency, and unbecoming conduct implied.	Not specified. —† Charges may be preferred by any interested party.		Hearing mentioned, but procedure not specified.—†Presentation of evidence by counsel.
Oregon	Gross dereliction of duty, or misconduct.	In writing, signed by person making them: presented to superintendent, or direct to board if superintendent will not transfer them.	Ten days.	Before board of directors; witnesses not exceeding ten allowed each party; teacher and board may use counsel; proceedings summary, board ruling on admitting evidence.
Wisconsin	Inefficiency, and immoral conduct, implied.	Written.	Ten days.	Before board,— † both parties being privileged to use witnesses and counsel.

¹ Information obtained from latest editions of the respective school codes.
† Interpretation or information was received from state department.

According to Table V, appeal from dismissal to higher educational authorities is allowed by five laws and to a special commission by one. This table shows appeal to regular law courts as being provided for in the indefinite tenure section of the education law of only one state, California, but in reality such appeal is possible in all but two states, Maryland and New York. Informa-

TABLE V
Appeal Procedures for Dismissed Teachers Provided in Existing Indefinite Tenure Laws[1]

State	Authority to Whom Appeal May Go	Type of Appeal	How Decided	Further Appeal
California	Superintendent of public instruction.	Direct to superintendent by dismissed employee, appeal being accompanied by two copies of reporter's record of hearing before local board.	On basis of reporter's record.	To court within sixty days from date of superintendent's decision.
Colorado	Law courts.†			
District of Columbia	Law courts.†			
Illinois	Law courts.†			
Indiana	County superintendent in case of decisions made by a township trustee. Decision of any city or town school board is termed final.	Made within ten days of date of township trustee's decision.	By investigation.	Any decision may be appealed to a law court for review.†
Louisiana				
Maryland	State superintendent of schools in cases where county board was not unanimous in its decisions. (This holds for suspension cases, also.)			Decision of state superintendent final.†
Massachusetts	Law courts, as evidenced by case records.			
Minnesota	Law courts, as evidenced by one case record.			

TABLE V—*Continued*

State	Authority to Whom Appeal May Go	Type of Appeal	How Decided	Further Appeal
New Jersey	State commissioner of education.[2]	Written statements and certified copies of documents may be required.	On basis of records and statements of aggrieved parties.	State board of education.
New York	Commissioner of education.[3]		On basis of evidence, as shown by records.	
Oregon	County commission of three, appointed annually by presiding judge of circuit court.	Written request within twenty days after board dismissal, stating type of hearing desired and whether counsel is to be used.	Upon evidence produced at hearing. Two of the three commissioners must concur in the decision.	To law courts if violation of contractual rights is claimed.†
Wisconsin	Law courts, as evidenced by case records.			

[1] Information obtained from latest editions of the respective school codes.
[2] Article II, Section 24, (10), School Laws of New Jersey, 1931, p. 15. Article VII, Section 165, XI (2), School Law, 1931, p. 86.
[3] Article 34, Sections 890, 891, and 892, Education Law, 1931, pp. 294–95.
† Interpretation or information was received from the state department.

tion on the nature of appeals and methods of deciding them is very inadequate; only four states mention the form of the appeal and five refer to the basis for decisions, this being records of cases or related records.

Six laws make no provisions for resignation of teachers, as shown in Table VI, although this is an important matter from the viewpoints of both the board and the teacher. Five of the seven laws which specify procedures require that resignations be in writing and six stipulate that a definite number of days' notice must be given the board.

Miscellaneous provisions are shown in Table VII, but, although numerous, none occurs frequently enough to merit consideration here.

TABLE VI
PROVISIONS FOR RESIGNATION IN EXISTING INDEFINITE TENURE LAWS[1]

State	Acting Body	Form Required	Number Days' Notice
California	Boards of school trustees; city, and city and county boards of education.		Not specified. Body acting sets time for resignation to take effect.
Colorado	Board of directors of a school district.[2]		Thirty days.
District of Columbia	Board of education.	In writing.†	Ten days.
Illinois			
Indiana	Governing body or official.	In writing.†	During school term, and thirty days previous thereto, resignation is possible only by mutual agreement. At any other time, five days' notice is sufficient.
Louisiana			
Maryland	County board of education.	Written notice.	Thirty days during June or July, except in case of emergency.
Massachusetts			
Minnesota			
New Jersey	Employing board of education.	Written notice.	Sixty days, unless board approves of shorter period.
New York			
Oregon	School board.[3]	In writing.	Sixty days before term begins. No other provision except in case of continued illness.
Wisconsin			

[1] Information obtained from latest editions of the respective school codes.
[2] Section 94, School Laws of the State of Colorado, 1927, pp. 65–66.
[3] Paragraph 35-2410, Chapter XXIV, School Laws of Oregon, 1931.

† Interpretation or information was received from the state department.

Analysis and Evaluation of Tenure Laws

TABLE VII
Miscellaneous Provisions of Existing Indefinite Tenure Laws[1]

State	Provisions
California	1. Certificated non-permanent employees must be classified as probationers. 2. Substitute employees serving in positions requiring certificated workers must be classified as substitutes. 3. Certificated employees, other than substitutes, serving first sixty days of term must be classified as temporary. If not dismissed during this time, they become probationary from beginning of service. 4. Notice of non-retention of probationary employee may be given on or before May 15. Must be delivered in person or by registered mail. 5. Probationary employees dismissible during school year only for cause. 6. No permanent employee shall be dismissed or deprived of his classification without his consent when district funds are insufficient to pay his salary. 7. No decrease in average daily attendance of a district can operate to deprive a permanent employee of his classification in said district. 8. Temporary and substitute employees may be dismissed at the pleasure of the board.
Colorado	Only general salary reductions applicable to salaries of fifty per cent or more of teachers in district are permissible. Salaries not reducible for political or religious reasons.
District of Columbia	1. Temporary suspension is without pay. 2. Salaries not reducible except by change in law.† 3. Transfers of educational employees without change of rank on recommendation of superintendent of schools.[2]
Illinois	1. Probationary employees dismissible by board upon recommendation of superintendent with reasons therefor in writing. 2. Teacher or principal promoted to assistant or district superintendent and then relieved of duties shall be reinstated in position from which promoted. 3. Past service of educational employees in system when law went into effect or who had been in system during the five years prior thereto, credited toward probationary requirement.
Indiana	1. Permanent status given any teacher with five years in a given system before the tenure law became effective and who was reëmployed thereafter. 2. Teachers' contracts may provide for annual fixing of salary amounts, which are changeable on or before May 1 of each year. Copies of new schedule must be given all teachers affected within thirty days of its adoption.

TABLE VII—*Continued*

State	Provisions
	3. Leaves of absence for one-year periods are available to permanent teachers for study or professional improvement, physical disability or sickness, if requested in writing. Such leave subject to rules of school corporation. 4. Corporation may put teacher on leave for not more than one year for physical or other disability or sickness, the teacher having right to hearing in such case.
Louisiana	All properly certificated teachers in system when law became effective accorded permanent status.
Maryland	Assignment and transfer left to county superintendent. If transfer is made during school year, it shall be done without loss of salary to employee.
Massachusetts	No teacher or superintendent lawfully dismissed shall receive compensation for services rendered thereafter or for any period of lawful suspension followed by dismissal.
Minnesota	1. No teacher dismissed for inefficiency unless charges are filed at least four months before the end of school year and discharge takes place during school year. 2. If charge against teacher is made by person not connected with school system, it may be disregarded by school board or commissioner. 3. Teachers dismissed for discontinuance of position or lack of pupils shall receive first consideration for other positions in their respective districts. 4. No loss of salary for temporary suspension if final decision is favorable to the teacher. 5. Teachers in districts when law became effective credited with prior years of service in computing probationary period.
New Jersey	Prior service of teachers in the several districts when law became effective counted in determining probationary requirements.
New York	1. Written report from superintendent or board of superintendents necessary at end of probationary period for permanent appointment. 2. Probationary employee dismissible on recommendation of superintendent or board of superintendents by majority vote of board of education; this action possible at any time. 3. Permanent teachers in cities having local indefinite tenure regulations when state law became effective retained their status. All teachers in cities not having local regulations were required to serve probationary periods set by their local boards.

TABLE VII—*Concluded*

State	Provisions
Oregon	1. Probationary teacher dismissible at any time for cause deemed sufficient by the board. If dismissal is to take effect at end of school year, teacher must be served with notice at least two and one-half months before said date. 2. No teacher or instructor may be dismissed for friction with principal before being given fair opportunity with another principal. 3. Transfers within a system possible if for good of service. Transfer to lower rank must be with consent of teacher or after hearing decided against teacher. No transfer affects teacher's standing as permanent employee. 4. Teachers in districts that lose identity as result of a merger retain rights as permanent teachers if probation periods are complete. 5. Subpœnaed witnesses for hearings are paid by persons having them called.
Wisconsin	Not any.

[1] Information obtained from latest editions of the respective school codes.
[2] Compilation of Laws Affecting the Public Schools, 1804–1929, District of Columbia, p. 34.
† Interpretation or information was received from the state department.

EVALUATION

The chief purpose of this section is to evaluate existing indefinite tenure laws in terms of the criteria which prevailed when a large majority, if not all, of them were legislated. Criteria presented were arrived at by a thorough review of educational literature on the subject; they embody all provisions for indefinite tenure laws on which there is or has been general agreement. Defects, or objectionable features, of these standards, are pointed out in connection with their exposition, but no changes are made.

Criteria

Comprehensive. An indefinite tenure law should apply in the same way to all districts in a state and to all educational employees concerned directly with classroom instruction.

Practically all printed statements concerning provisions desirable for an indefinite tenure law either declare definitely or imply that the scope of the law should be state-wide. Vanatta[2] states unequivocally that a law should apply to all districts of a state

[2] Vanatta, H. E., "A Study of Existing and Proposed Tenure Laws." In Ms. (1924).

and Housman[3] likewise holds that this is a desirable feature. The obvious advantage of such a provision is that it protects teachers wherever they are, regardless of variations in administrative practices or attitudes of school officials. The main objection is that it does not take into account real differences existing among districts of different types.

As for the application of a law to educational employees, it appears reasonable that, wherever it applies at all, it should include all workers whose main concern is classroom instruction, i.e., teachers, principals, and supervisors. Cubberley[4] suggests that it is probably best to classify principals and supervisors as teachers; and the National Education Association[5] avers that all classes of certificated employees should be protected on the status of a teacher, at least. According to the consensus of opinion, administrators *per se* (superintendents, assistant superintendents, etc.) should not be given indefinite tenure. Cubberley (*supra*[4]) holds that the superintendent should have a measure of security, his work being subject to review and evaluation regularly, and proposes a five-year term for this officer. In criticism of the ideas in this paragraph, it may be said that application of a law to all educational employees regardless of the certificates held is probably unwise. If protected tenure were granted only to employees who hold certificates of the highest or next to the highest grade, a more salutary effect on the efficiency of the teaching personnel might well be expected.

Assures Competent Educational Personnel. An indefinite teacher tenure law should provide protection only for properly certificated teachers who have completed a definite and adequate period of probationary service.

That teachers should possess at least the state minimum training requirements for the positions they hold before becoming eligible for tenure protection, there seems to be no doubt. Kandel[6] gives this as one of the premises upon which safeguarded tenure should be based and other authorities concur in this view. The National Education Association (*supra*[5]) holds that indefinite tenure should

---

[3] Housman, Ida E., "Tenure Once More," *Ed. Rev.*, Vol. 68, pp. 118-22, Oct. 1924.
[4] Cubberley, E. P., *State School Administration*, p. 650.
[5] *N.E.A. Addresses and Proc.*, 1930, Vol. 68, p. 196.
[6] Kandel, I. L., "Tenure of Service for Teachers," *Teachers College Record*, Vol. 26, No. 3, p. 142, Oct. 1924.

Analysis and Evaluation of Tenure Laws 43

be granted only upon evidence of satisfactory preliminary training, successful experience, and professional growth. This statement embraces everything contained in the criterion under discussion and, like the criterion itself, is general in character. "Proper certification," as the writer sees it and as pointed out above, should probably not mean merely legal certificates but rather certificates of the higher ranks. In this evaluation, however, it will be taken as meaning any kind of acceptable certificate.

Universal agreement prevails concerning the necessity for a probationary period, although there is not unanimity of opinion as to the most desirable length. The periods suggested most frequently are three years and two to three years. Almack and Lang[7] suggest the second and maintain that the beginning teacher should be given opportunity to serve with more than one principal before being dropped for inefficiency or incompetency. Weak features of the probationary requirement as commonly proposed, or at least some that may be regarded as such, are that it seems to be for the purpose of determining the efficiency of old and new teachers instead of for training beginners; it makes no provision for transference of teachers with full or partial credit given for prior service; and it makes impossible extension of the trial period when this may be warranted.

Another weakness of the criterion under discussion is that it makes no provision for insuring the continued efficiency of teachers during extended service. Perhaps a law should not in itself make such provisions, but it should at least give local systems the privilege of setting up reasonable regulations.

Facilitates Administration of Educational Personnel. An indefinite tenure law should facilitate or at least not hinder in any way good personnel practices.

Inherent in the major thesis of indefinite tenure is the implication that school administrators shall be free to employ personnel practices that conserve the best interests of the school. In other words, a school system should be able to transfer, suspend, or dismiss an educational employee when either the teacher or the pupils concerned, or both, would be benefited by the change. Transfers within school systems, involving either promotions or demotions, should certainly be permissible, and Kandel[8] claims that teachers

---
[7] Almack, John C. and Lang, A. R., *Problems of the Teaching Profession*, p. 231.
[8] Footnote Ref. No. 6, p. 143.

should not lose their status when transferred from one district to another in the same state. Cubberley[9] suggests that transferred teachers be given credit for satisfactory service elsewhere up to three-fifths of the length of the probationary period required; while Vanatta (*supra*[2]) states that it might be well to require ordinarily a single year of probation of a transferred teacher, allowing opportunity, however, for transfer without change of status.

Common consent and sound logic both recommend that disciplinary powers be vested in the employing board and that this body have the right to suspend teachers pending dismissal proceedings and to dismiss for stated causes. With regard to dismissal, the National Education Association (*supra*[5]) holds that provision should be made for easy removal of unsatisfactory or incompetent teachers for clearly demonstrable causes. There seems to be reason enough for claiming that temporary suspension might well be used as a disciplinary measure after charges have been proved, but there is not enough support for this to include it in the criterion.

A final feature of the criterion which is generally accepted is that teachers should be required to give reasonable notice in writing before resigning a position. An addition which the writer considers necessary is a requirement that teachers who continue in service after retirement age shall do so at the pleasure of the board. This implies the existence of retirement laws where indefinite tenure laws operate, a condition which is not always present, although the two should be coexistent.

Guarantees Teachers Just Treatment. Teachers' rights should be guaranteed by opportunity to remedy deficiencies in teaching, by definitely outlined and fair disciplinary procedures, and by provision for appeal from decisions of local boards.

The justice of allowing incompetent and inefficient teachers a chance to improve after their shortcomings have been pointed out seems readily apparent. Almack and Lang (*supra*[7]) give this as a necessary provision of an indefinite tenure law or of an ancillary personnel practice, but confine their recommendations to the pro-

---

[9] Footnote Ref. No. 4, p. 648.

Analysis and Evaluation of Tenure Laws 45

bationary teacher. Cubberley[10] thinks it would be well to place unsatisfactory teachers, regardless of their service records, on probation for one year. Details of such matters might well be left to local administrative authorities, but the requirement probably should be a part of an indefinite tenure law.

Dismissal proceedings should be initiated and carried out according to this outline: (1) preferring of written charges; (2) notification of teacher; (3) arrangement for hearing within stated time if desired by teacher; (4) hearing before board with accused and board privileged to have witnesses and counsel; (5) dismissal by formal action of board with teacher given due notice. The general opinion on the subject of charges seems to be that they should be presented by the superintendent or the governing board. This, however, does not prohibit filing of charges by any interested party through the superintendent of schools. The accused teacher should be allowed a definite length of time in which to answer the charges and request a hearing, which may be public or private. Always the board or a specially authorized committee of the same should hold the hearing. Kandel[11] defends the right of the teacher to have counsel and it may be inferred that the board should also be thus privileged. Causes for dismissal should be stated in a law, and provision should be made for the giving of formal notice to dismissed teachers by the governing boards.

Right of appeal to state educational authorities from dismissal decisions of local boards is almost universally accepted. Cubberley (*supra*[10]) upholds such appeal, but maintains that resort to the courts should be had only when a teacher's rights as defined in the law are infringed, since the dismissal of a teacher is an educational and not a legal question. No well-defined opinion exists concerning the right of a dismissed teacher to appeal to the law courts; however, it is generally known that she may bring suit for violation of contractual rights.

Application of Criteria

Judged by the standards developed in the preceding section, existing indefinite tenure laws are decidedly incomplete and inadequate. This is shown in concrete form by Table VIII, which is a check list for application of the criteria. The checks entered are

[10] Footnote Ref. No. 4, pp. 648-49.
[11] Footnote Ref. No. 6, p. 144.

TABLE VIII

APPLICATION OF CRITERIA TO EXISTING INDEFINITE TEACHER TENURE LAWS[1]

Criteria	Cal.	Col.	D.C.	Ill.	Ind.	La.	Md.	Mass.	Minn.	N.J.	N.Y.	Ore.	Wis.
1. Comprehensive.													
a. Universally applicable as to districts, *i.e.*, state-wide		✓		✓					✓				
b. Protects all educational employees concerned directly with classroom procedure	✓	✓	✓	✓	✓	✓	✓	✓	✓	✓	✓	✓	✓
2. Assures Competent Educational Personnel.													
a. Proper teacher's certificate required for protection	✓	✓	✓	✓	✓	✓	✓	✓	✓	✓	✓	✓	✓
b. Probationary period of two to three years followed by indefinite appointment	✓	✓		✓		✓	✓	✓	✓	✓	✓	✓	
3. Facilitates Administration of Educational Personnel.													
a. Provides for transfers within systems			✓				✓				✓		
b. Disciplinary authority vested in employing board	✓	✓	✓	✓	✓	✓	✓	✓	✓	✓	✓	✓	✓
c. Provides for temporary suspension pending dismissal proceedings	✓			✓	✓	✓			✓	✓	✓	✓	
d. Provides dismissal for stated causes	✓	✓			✓	✓	✓			✓	✓	✓	
e. Requires written resignations and fixed number of days' notice		✓					✓			✓		✓	
4. Guarantees Teachers Just Treatment.													
a. Provides for warning of unsatisfactory teachers with opportunity for improvement												✓	
b. States manner in which charges must be preferred	✓	✓	✓	✓			✓	✓		✓		✓	✓
c. States time for answering of charges and requesting hearing		✓			✓	✓		✓	✓	✓		✓	✓
d. Provides for hearing as matter of course or upon request	✓	✓	✓	✓	✓	✓	✓	✓	✓	✓	✓	✓	✓
e. Prescribes general nature of hearing, at least	✓	✓	✓	✓	✓			✓	✓	✓		✓	✓
f. Requires written board decision within stated time after hearing													
g. Provides for appeal to higher educational authorities	✓				✓		✓			✓	✓		
State totals (total possible score, 16)	10	8	11	9	11	7	12	8	10	12	6	13	8
Percentages of total possible	62	50	69	56	69	44	75	50	62	75	38	81	50

[1] Criteria arrived at by a study of educational literature on the subject. Checks based on data concerning the laws presented in this chapter.

based on all information presented in Tables II–VII, in the present chapter, rather than on obvious interpretations of the statutes commonly regarded to be the tenure laws of the various states. Had this policy not been followed, the laws would have appeared considerably more deficient. Taken as a whole, they are only 60 per cent perfect (counting all items as equal in value); and the range is from 38 to 81 per cent perfect. Provisions omitted most frequently from the laws are these: (1) state-wide application;

Analysis and Evaluation of Tenure Laws

(2) transfer regulations; (3) requirement of written resignation and time notice; (4) warning of unsatisfactory teachers and opportunity for improvement; (5) written board decision after hearing with time limit fixed; and (6) appeal to higher educational authorities.

This criterial evaluation is valuable mainly for demonstrating omissions of the several statutes; it merely shows which of the supposedly fundamental provisions are included in each of the laws and disregards altogether the factor of sufficiency. Consequently, it affords only an incomplete basis for comparison of the laws with one another, although it does place the statutes in somewhat correct order, according to general professional estimate.

An example of the inadequacy of the criteria is to be found in the respective scores for the California and New Jersey laws. The former is much more detailed than the latter, is obviously better framed than the latter, yet it received a lower rating. Similarly, the District of Columbia law scored higher than that of California despite the fact that no section of the school code of the District can be termed a tenure law. The shortcomings of the evaluation, however, do not in any sense invalidate it as a measure of the inclusiveness of the laws taken either singly or together.

SUMMARY

Most important of the general characteristics of protective tenure laws as revealed by the analysis and criterial evaluation presented in this chapter, are indefinite wording of provisions and incompleteness of the laws. Twenty-three items appearing in the tabular analysis are based on interpretations and supplementary information received from the state departments of education represented and fourteen others were taken from related provisions of the respective education laws. Omissions are ordinarily justified when other sections of the education law adequately cover the points in question, a condition not always found, but there is no excuse for vagueness or indefinite wording of statutes.

Only two laws are state-wide in application; the others range from state-wide application except in the case of a single city to application to one city alone. The only provisions common to all statutes are as follows: (1) protection for all employees concerned directly with classroom instruction; (2) fixed probation period; (3) proper certification required for teaching; (4) disciplinary authority vested in board; and (5) hearings held as a matter of routine or upon request. Failure of specific tenure sections in seven cases to make any mention of educational qualifications for teaching appears to be a serious defect; likewise the omission from five laws of specific causes for dismissal and from eight laws of a provision for appeal from dismissal to higher educational authorities may be deemed inexcusable.

Criteria used in judging the laws were developed by a study of educational literature and are as follows: (1) comprehensive—applies to all districts in a state and to all instructional personnel; (2) assures competent educational personnel; (3) facilitates administration of educational personnel; and (4) guarantees teachers just treatment.

These principles are inadequate in a number of respects, but they represent the best thought on indefinite tenure during the period when practically all existing laws were enacted. Application of the criteria to the laws served to emphasize the general deficiency or incompleteness demonstrated by the tabular analysis; for, taken together, the statutes rate only 60 per cent of perfect, the lowest percentage score being 38 and the highest 81. The weakest feature of the criterial judgment is that it fails to show the sufficiency of provisions, i.e., the adequacy, but simply records their inclusion or absence.

SELECTED REFERENCES

CALIFORNIA. *School Code of the State of California,* 1931. Office of Superintendent of Public Instruction, Sacramento, Calif.

DISTRICT OF COLUMBIA. *Laws Affecting Public Schools, 1804-1929.* United States Government Printing Office, Washington, D. C., 1929.

———. *Manual for Teachers.* Board of Education, District of Columbia, 1931.

ILLINOIS. *The School Law of Illinois.* Circular No. 256. State Superintendent of Public Instruction, Springfield, Ill., 1931.

INDIANA. *Burn's Annotated Statutes, Watson's Revision, Supplement of 1929.* The Bobbs-Merrill Company, Indianapolis, Ind., 1929.

LOUISIANA. *Louisiana State School Code.* State Department of Education, Baton Rouge, La., 1931.

MARYLAND. *Maryland Public School Laws,* 1927. State Department of Education, Baltimore, Md.

MASSACHUSETTS. *General Laws Relating to Education, The Common-*

wealth of Massachusetts. Bulletin of the Department of Education, 1927, No. 4, Boston, Mass.

MINNESOTA. *Mason's Minnesota Statutes,* Vol. I. Citer Digest Company, Saint Paul, Minn., 1927.

NEW JERSEY. *New Jersey School Laws.* Commissioner of Education, Trenton, N. J., 1931.

NEW YORK. *University of the State of New York,* Bulletin No. 978. State Education Department, Albany, N. Y., 1931.

OREGON. *School Laws of Oregon,* 1931. Superintendent of Public Instruction, Salem, Ore.

WISCONSIN. *Wisconsin Statutes,* 1929. (Edited by E. E. Brossard, Revisor.) State of Wisconsin, Madison, Wis.

CHAPTER IV

Operation of Indefinite Teacher Tenure Laws

MUCH that has been written on the question of effects of indefinite teacher tenure statutes has been based on subjective opinion and colored considerably by the enthusiasm of the writers. The inherent difficulty of measuring actual results has been partly responsible for this dependence on dialectical argument; but a crusading spirit on the part of sponsors of indefinite tenure can alone be credited with the lack of caution shown. It is the purpose of this chapter both to evaluate critically the claims that have been made for protective tenure and to point out the main features of its real operative effects.

Principal claims made for the practice are as follows:

1. It provides for easy dismissal of incompetent, inefficient, or insubordinate teachers.
2. It protects teachers from political, social, or other unprofessional attacks.
3. It relieves teachers of anxiety over possibility of failure to secure reëlection.
4. It decreases turnover, or stabilizes the profession.
5. It attracts able and competent people to the profession (by increasing its dignity and safety).
6. It encourages professional growth; increases fidelity, efficiency, and initiative.

EVALUATION OF MAJOR CLAIMS FOR INDEFINITE TENURE

Two-thirds of the principal claims for protected tenure cannot be proved true and practically all of these, along with the remaining one-third, the validity of which cannot be questioned, resolve themselves, either singly or in groups, into problems that have yet to be solved. These problems are peculiar to indefinite tenure in some cases, but in others are common to the field of teacher personnel in general.

Dismissal of Undesirable Teachers

Removal from office of undesirable teachers, indefinite tenure enthusiasts to the contrary notwithstanding, is ordinarily difficult under any protective tenure law and may be regarded as the crux of the whole situation. This conclusion is supported by all the data obtained on the subject except those taken from published comments, which present rather evenly divided opinions, and from the records of appeal cases for Massachusetts. Claims that dismissal of indefinite tenure teachers for cause is easily accomplished take the form of simple, declarative statements such as the following:

> Through tenure the good teachers will be left undisturbed in their positions, while the weak and inefficient will be obliged to look elsewhere for positions.[1]

The opposite viewpoint is typified by an opinion expressed by Broome:[2]

> I should say that the chief danger of this law [New Jersey] is that it results in lodgment in office rather than in tenure of office. That is to say, the means of removing a teacher for anything but immoral conduct is so difficult that a superintendent will permit mediocre teachers to remain undisturbed year after year rather than to take steps toward removal.[2]

Holmstedt's study[3] revealed that dismissal of unsatisfactory teachers is the greatest and most aggravating problem New Jersey officials have to face as a result of the indefinite tenure law. He holds the statute at fault for making dismissal difficult. In New York, city superintendents recently reported in a questionnaire study that removal of undesirable teachers was not reasonably possible.[4] The difficulty of dismissal in Oregon is witnessed by the fact that from July 1, 1913, to November 1927, only fourteen elementary teachers in Portland were brought to trial under the

---

[1] Scattergood, Mrs. Joseph, "Teacher Tenure from the School Director's Viewpoint," *American School Board Journal*, Vol. 78, No. 5, p. 130, May 1929.

[2] Broome, E. C., "Advantages and Disadvantages of the Permanent Tenure Law in New Jersey," *University of Pa. 9th Annual Schoolmen's Week Proceedings*, 1922, pp. 226-27.

[3] Holmstedt, Raleigh W., *A Study of the Effects of the Teacher Tenure Law in New Jersey*, pp. 100-01.

[4] Dodge, H. S., "Desirable Changes in the Teacher Tenure Law," *Bulletin of the Associated School Boards and Trustees of the State of N. Y.*, Vol. 3, No. 2, pp. 7-9, June 1931.

indefinite tenure law;[5] and five of these were reinstated. Investigations made by the writer of the operation of the Illinois, Minnesota, and New Jersey laws afford further evidence of the type just cited.

During the twelve-year period, 1920-1931, inclusive, only fourteen educational workers were dismissed in Chicago and but twenty-three others were subjected to less severe disciplinary action.[6] Nine of the employees dismissed had permanent status and the others were probationers. In 1927 Superintendent William McAndrew rendered a comparative report on dismissals to the board of education, listing ten dismissals as the total for the seven years immediately preceding.[7] He observed at the outset that dismissal is contrary to a time-honored Chicago tradition and that almost no removals for incompetency occur. Later he commented on the dismissal of only four teachers in a given year in this wise:

> But it seems incredible that only three one-hundredths of one per cent. out of 12,000 teachers, indicate the number whom the Board should separate from the service on the ground of inefficiency. The law evidently intended an early relief from unsatisfactory service.[7]

Minnesota cities have also had extremely few cases of dismissal since the passage of the state law. Duluth reported no removals from service.[8] Board of education records for Minneapolis show only four dismissals, none of which was appealed. Saint Paul reported severance of relations with only six to ten teachers, all of whom were evidently probationers.

> In most cases teachers have resigned of their own accord; there have not been more than two or three cases where we have given formal notice of discontinuance. We have had no cases of dismissal after hearing for any of the causes established by the law for consideration of charges against permanent appointees.[9]

The two New Jersey cities visited by the writer, i.e., Newark and Trenton, had together dismissed only one teacher during the five-year period ending June 1931, this removal having occurred in Newark.

Three state departments, viz., those of California, Oregon, and

---

[5] "Status of the Elementary Teacher," p. 8. Ore. State Teachers Ass'n., Jan. 1928.
[6] Data from Proceedings of the Board of Ed., Chicago, Ill.
[7] Board Proceedings, Chicago, Ill., March 23, 1927, pp. 1326-327.
[8] Letter from Leonard Young, Supt. of Schs., under date Nov. 24, 1931.
[9] Letter from S. O. Hartwell, Supt. of Schs., under date Dec. 21, 1931.

Operation of Tenure Laws

Wisconsin, reported upon inquiry that removal of the inefficient teacher is a real problem under their laws.

Protection from Unjustified Attacks and Anxiety Regarding Retention

That teachers serving under indefinite tenure laws are, in the main, protected against unjustified attacks, whether political or personal, and from anxiety concerning the safety of their positions, there appears to be no question. Evidence set forth in the preceding section constitutes adequate proof of this. Degrees of protection afforded by the several laws vary to some extent; however, protection of teachers' interests, which Holmstedt (*supra*[3]) demonstrated to be the major value of the New Jersey law, is undoubtedly the chief merit or characteristic of all the statutes.

One of the weakest of the several state laws from the standpoint of security afforded teachers, is the Massachusetts law. Partial proof of this is found in statements appearing from time to time in *Common Ground*, the official publication of the Massachusetts Teachers' Federation. In 1920 the annual report of the Tenure Committee called attention to the defects of the law and stated that some members of the Federation considered it of no value so far as making a teacher's tenure permanent was concerned.[10] An editorial published in 1922 pointed out the prevalence of dismissal at that time and the evident ease with which local officials could dispense with the services of educational employees.[11] Another editorial protest against the limited protection of the law reads thus:

> Tenure has been given to all other State and municipal employees, but those most faithful and hard working public servants—teachers—have no tenure worthy of the name.[12]

Further and more reliable proof of the weakness of the Massachusetts law appears in the records of teacher tenure appeal cases for the state, which are studied in Chapter V.

Stabilization of the Profession

Reduction in teacher turnover has long been claimed for indefinite tenure—and the tendency may be in this direction—but

---
[10] "Legislative Program for 1920," *Common Ground*, Vol. 1, No. 13, p. 5, April 1920.
[11] "Removal for Cause" (Ed.), *Common Ground*, Vol. 2, No. 8, p. 136, Oct. 1922.
[12] "Tenure" (Ed.), *Common Ground*, Vol. 2, No. 2, p. 39, April 1921.

proof has thus far been lacking. The following statement may be termed typical of published comment with respect to this point:

> One thing seems certain that where tenure legislation is in force teacher turnover is reduced and teachers are not so liable to use the profession as a stepping stone to another line of work.[13]

Research studies that have touched on this matter indicate that guaranteed tenure does not *ipso facto* reduce turnover. Elsbree,[14] for instance, found that there was no significant difference between the rate of unavoidable turnover in villages not included in the New York tenure law and in comparable cities in which the law applies. Holmstedt (*supra*[3]) reported some slight evidence that the New Jersey law has been a stabilizing factor, but qualified this by calling attention to other factors operating here. Turnover is unquestionably a function, not of insecurity alone, but also of variations in positions, in salaries, in personal desires, and the like.

Drawing Power of Profession and Professional Improvement of Teachers

Although security of tenure should make the teaching profession more attractive and should tend to make teachers more professional, demonstrable improvements in these respects could not in any case be ascribed to indefinite tenure alone. This error was made by the Tenure Committee of the National Education Association in its report for 1927, wherein it attempted to prove statistically that protective tenure laws make the profession more attractive to capable young people. Other important influencing factors such as the rising salary trend at that time and increasing competition in other occupational fields were ignored altogether. And this effort is the only one that has been made to study the effects of protective tenure upon the drawing power of the profession.

With regard to interest in professional improvement, Holmstedt (*supra*[3]) found that New Jersey teachers do not differ from unprotected teachers.

CERTAIN OTHER INDEFINITE TENURE PROBLEMS

Questions to be taken up in this division, like those of the preceding one, belong in some instances peculiarly to the province of indefinite tenure and in others to the general field of teacher

---
[13] Scattergood, *op. cit.*
[14] Elsbree, W. S., *Teacher Turnover in Cities and Villages of New York State,* pp. 65 ff.

personnel. The latter type, though, present different aspects in states having indefinite tenure laws and consequently call for different treatment.

Probationary Periods

Evidence secured in this study indicates that inflexible probationary periods rather frequently work hardships on teachers. The main device used for evading the provisions of indefinite tenure laws in five states, Massachusetts, Minnesota, Indiana, Oregon, and Wisconsin, according to information received from the state departments of education in these states, is refusal to grant a teacher permanent status at the end of a trial period of service. This device is also employed to some extent in New York (*supra*[4]) and is commonly used in New Jersey.[15]

It is probable, moreover, that the general tendency is to treat probation as a routine matter or as a period for judging, rather than as an opportunity to give novices needed training. Judgment is about all that could take place in Chicago under the "short-circuit" arrangement reported by Dix.[16] Instead of serving three years of probation, as required by law, new teachers actually serve two short probationary periods totaling four months in length. Permanent status is not granted until the end of the third year, but the critical period of testing ends with the fourth month.

Rural Teacher Problem

At least two of the five states having indefinite tenure laws which apply in country districts have found that rural teachers constitute a special problem. Bessac[17] found that the California law in force in 1928 was operating less satisfactorily in the country districts than in the cities. Rural opposition to guaranteed tenure was doubtless responsible for the revision of the California law in 1931, with the result that application of the statute in districts having less than 850 A.D.A. is optional with the school trustees or governing officials.

Indiana has experienced considerable difficulty in getting trustees

---

[15] Records of Committee on Grievances and Redress, New Jersey State Teachers' Association.

[16] Dix, Lester, "The Educational Personnel of the Schools," *Report of the Survey of the Schools of Chicago, Illinois*, Vol. 1, p. 293, 1932.

[17] Bessac, Harry, "How the Tenure Law Is Working," *Sierra Ed. News*, Vol. 24, No. 10, pp. 16-17, Dec. 1928.

of rural schools to accept the indefinite tenure law. A recent questionnaire study made by the School of Education, University of Indiana, shows only 13.58 per cent of the rural teachers in sixty-four counties as having permanent status while 38.66 per cent of the teachers in the 131 cities reporting have permanent rank. Furthermore, the counties reported that 8.68 per cent of their educational personnel had been discharged or not reappointed on account of the indefinite tenure law as against .68 per cent for the cities. The existence of the rural problem has been frankly acknowledged from time to time in the *Indiana Teacher*, the official publication of the Indiana Teachers' Association, but no suggestion has been made for solving it except more rigid application of the tenure law. A characteristic comment with respect to this point follows:

> In spite of the rural opposition to Indiana's new tenure law, and in some cases because of it, one of the greatest needs of the country schools of Indiana today is the assurance that tenure protection will be given to all competent and well-qualified rural teachers. Those trustees who refuse to make the tenure law operative in their townships are standing in the way of educational progress.[18]

Transfers and Resignations

These two problems are considered together since they are somewhat commonly used in indefinite tenure states as devices for avoidance of outright dismissal of unsatisfactory teachers. In Chicago, Illinois, for instance, inefficient teachers are usually given the benefit of the doubt that they might do better in other schools and accordingly are transferred.[19] Physically and mentally unfit members of this group, however, are ordinarily urged to resign. Newark, New Jersey, teachers who receive the grade of "unsatisfactory" in official ratings are frequently disposed of through the mediums of transfer and resignation. Of the 274 teachers who were given this grade in the June semiannual ratings from 1927-1931, inclusive, forty were given changes of assignment and fifty-two resigned.[20] Only one of the total number was dismissed, seven retired, and four were granted furloughs; the remaining 170 evidently improved sufficiently in their original positions to be retained. Probationary teachers make up the bulk of the unsatis-

[18] "Rural Schools and Tenure" (Ed.), *Ind. Teacher*, Vol. 73, No. 6, p. 16, Jan. 1929.
[19] Board Proceedings, Chicago, Ill., March 23, 1927, p. 1326.
[20] Private Records, Office of Supt. of Ed., Newark, N. J.

Operation of Tenure Laws

factory group in Newark. Whether probationary or permanent, Newark teachers who apparently cannot render satisfactory service are advised to resign; and a similar condition holds for Trenton, New Jersey, probationary teachers. Resignation as an alternative to dismissal is also to be found in Minnesota: Duluth has requested two teachers of permanent rank to resign in order to avoid dismissal proceedings since the state law went into effect (*supra*[8]), and Saint Paul reports that teachers who have been separated from the service have, generally speaking, resigned of their own volition (*supra*[9]).

Difficulty in effecting transfers involving demotions was reported to the writer by the state departments of New Jersey and New York.

Salary and Retirement Policies

Five states and the District of Columbia have indefinite tenure regulations which offer either potential or actual obstacles to changes in salary policies, that is, to reductions. In the District of Columbia, salaries can be reduced only by congressional action; the New Jersey indefinite tenure law has a mandatory provision prohibiting reduction of individual salaries; Colorado and Indiana can reduce in only a general way; Minnesota reported that the law might offer hindrance to budget reductions; and Wisconsin admitted that its statute presents something of a problem in this respect.

The close relation between retirement and indefinite tenure provisions, from a practical administrative standpoint, was well demonstrated by an attempt of the Chicago Board of Education to establish emeritus service for teachers who had attained seventy years of age. "Emeritus" rules adopted December 9, 1925, provided *inter alia* that "hereafter no member of the teaching force shall be continued in classroom or supervisory duties who shall be more than seventy years of age." Teachers transferred to this new branch of the service were to be subject to the call of the superintendent or board for consultation, advice, or other such service as required; and were to receive an annual salary equal to one-half of their average annual salary for the preceding ten years, provided this was not less than $1,500 or greater than $2,500. But the board was enjoined from enforcing its emeritus, or retirement, rules by the Appellate Court of Illinois, which held in Armstrong v. Chicago[21] that the board was without legal authority to pass such rules, that the services required of emeritus teachers were so slight as to indicate bad faith or subterfuge, and that teachers who had been transferred should be reinstated and paid the respective amounts of salary lost. Teachers represented in the case just cited were eligible for retirement under the Miller act of 1925, but could not have been forced to retire under this act until 1929.

Miscellaneous Problems

Married women teachers seem to constitute a problem in several, and perhaps in all, of the indefinite tenure states. City superintendents in New York State who coöperated in a recent questionnaire study of tenure are of the opinion that permanent status should terminate with marriage (supra[4]); and in New Jersey alleged discrimination against married women teachers is an important cause of tenure disputes (supra[15]).

Restricted application and indefinite wording of certain of the laws were pointed out in Chapter II as deficiencies. The California law of 1921 was criticized on these bases[22] and the original Massachusetts law was considered to be lacking in essential features.

According to information received from the state departments of education, temporary suspension as a disciplinary measure is permissible in California, the District of Columbia, and Maryland; it is forbidden in Colorado, Indiana, Minnesota, and New Jersey. No reports on this question were received from the six other states included in this study.

A final problem worthy of mention is the tendency of some school administrative officials to ignore or evade indefinite tenure statutes. Recently an editorial in the *Indiana Teacher* credited much of the objection to the Indiana law to lack of familiarity with its provisions and prescribed procedures on the part of those administering it.[23] Attempts to evade ruling statutes have been mentioned in other sections of this chapter, e.g., dropping of probationers to avoid granting of permanent status, requested resignations, and so forth.

---

[21] Armstrong v. Chicago, 159 N. E. 217 (1928).
[22] "Adequate Tenure Laws Benefit Schools," *American Schoolmaster*, Vol. 16, pp. 112-14, Nov. 15, 1923.
[23] "Two Observations on Teacher Tenure" (Ed.), *Ind. Teacher*, Vol. 76, No. 2, p. 18, Oct. 1931.

TENURE AND RELATED CASES ARISING UNDER THE ILLINOIS AND NEW JERSEY LAWS

This section presents detailed facts concerning tenure and related cases arising under the Illinois law during the twelve-year period 1920-1931, inclusive, and of a large percentage of such cases occurring in New Jersey during the six-year period 1926-1931. Incidentally or by implication, this information will serve further to illustrate certain of the major and minor problems of indefinite tenure. Data for Illinois were obtained from the Proceedings of the Board of Education of Chicago (the only school system in which the law applies) and for New Jersey from the private records of the Committee on Grievances and Redress of the State Teachers' Association.[24] It is the province of this Committee to investigate the legal status of teachers who are in contest with educational authorities in relation to their rights and render legal and financial aid, under the direction of the Executive Committee of the Association.[25]

Chicago, Illinois

Dismissals occurring in Chicago during the twelve-year period in question are presented in Table IX and minor disciplinary cases for the same period, with the disposition thereof, are shown in Table X. Both tables segregate cases according to type and show the status of the teachers involved. Overlappings among the types are due to the similarity of charges made by the board of education and to the use of these charges by the writer for designation of types. Only five of the fourteen teachers dismissed were probationers as compared to twenty of the twenty-three who suffered minor disciplinary action.

Unsatisfactory service as a teacher, inefficiency, and incompetency account for a majority of the dismissal cases and also for almost one-half of the minor disciplinary cases. Insubordination with other aggravating conditions account for the remainder of the dismissal cases and for several of the remaining cases in Table

---

[24] These esoteric documents, consisting largely of letters and minutes of meetings, were made available to the writer through the kindness of Miss Adelaide E. Davis, Secretary of the Committee, with the approval of the Committee.

[25] Article XIX of the By-Laws, Constitution of the New Jersey State Teachers' Association.

TABLE IX
Teacher Dismissal Cases Occurring in Chicago from 1920–1931, Inclusive[1]

Nature of Case	Probationary	Permanent	Total
Unsatisfactory service, inefficiency, and incompetency	5	4	9
Insubordination and inefficiency	--	2	2
Insubordination and unbecoming conduct	--	1	1
Insubordination and unpatriotic conduct, particularly on Nov. 11, 1920	--	1	1
Insubordination, unbecoming conduct, administration of corporal punishment, violation of rules and regulations	--	1	1
Total	5	9	14

[1] Data obtained from the Proceedings of the Board of Education for the period covered.

X. Violation of a debt rule established by the board of education, providing for suspension of a teacher for debt delinquencies, is the second most important cause for minor disciplinary action, while variations of unsatisfactory service or unbecoming conduct comprise the remaining cases. Nine of the minor disputes solved themselves by voluntary resignation of the teachers concerned; six were disposed of by temporary suspension; and the remainder were divided equally among transfers, recommendations for transfer, leaves of absence, and withdrawal of charges.

Charges brought against Chicago teachers take the form of simple declarative statements that name general shortcomings rather than specific acts. According to the tenure law, charges must be preferred by the superintendent of schools; but any interested party may present charges to the superintendent of schools.[26] The validity of charges is determined by the board on the basis of evidence presented. No rules exist for guidance here and board records of cases ordinarily do not give the evidence adduced in support of charges. Consequently, no controlling principles for interpretation of the common charges, i.e., inefficiency, incompetency, insubordination, and unbecoming conduct, emerge from the writer's investigation. It should be noted, however, that inefficiency or incompetency was charged against one

[26] Letter from J. A. Lindsay, Asst. to the Dir. of the Chicago Survey, under date April 4, 1932.

TABLE X

MINOR TEACHER DISCIPLINARY CASES IN CHICAGO, 1920–1931, INCLUSIVE, AND DISPOSITION THEREOF[1]

Nature of Case	Number		Disposition					
	Probationary	Permanent	Voluntary Resignation	Temporary Suspension	Transfer	Transfer Recommended	Leave of Absence	Charges Withdrawn
Unsatisfactory service, inefficiency, and incompetency	9	2	6	--	2	2	1	--
Debt delinquency — violation of board rule regarding such	4	--	1	3	--	--	--	--
Conduct unbecoming of a teacher; conduct destroying efficiency as a teacher	3	--	1	2	--	--	--	--
Incompetency, insubordination, unbecoming conduct	1	--	1	--	--	--	--	--
Insubordination and inefficiency	1	--	--	1	--	--	--	--
Insubordination	1	--	--	--	--	--	--	1
Neglect of duty, insubordination, unbecoming conduct	1	--	--	--	--	--	--	1
Unsatisfactory service, non-coöperativeness, poor discipline, and administration of corporal punishment	--	1	--	--	--	--	1	--
Total	20	3	9	6	2	2	2	2

[1] Data obtained from the Proceedings of the Board of Education for the period covered.

teacher because her pupils had "failed to show results of efficient instruction as compared with other pupils of the same grade";[27] and another was found guilty for inefficiency and incompetency because

> [she] insisted on following antiquated and obsolete methods of teaching contrary to the modern, accepted standard methods generally used in educational circles and prescribed in the Chicago Public School System; classroom work was conducted in a mechanical manner with no ability on Miss ———'s part to arouse the interest of the pupils in their work; her recitations were conducted in a loose and purposeless manner; her pupils constantly failed in geography, writing, spelling, grammar, and arithmetic tests given to determine whether or not Miss ——— was efficiently teaching such subjects to them.[28]

Principals in Chicago, and perhaps other school officials, render reports from time to time on the efficiency of teachers. Special consideration is then evidently given weak or unsatisfactory teachers. This conclusion is drawn from the following excerpt from a report of the Superintendent of Schools:

> In accordance with the Law [Sec. 161] I have examined the records of teachers reported as not rendering satisfactory service.
> I have interviewed personally thirty-three and am prepared to submit written charges required in the case of teachers who have served more than the probationary period of three years, such teachers being entitled to a trial by the Board and I am prepared also to present the cases of teachers serving less than a period of three years whose services the Board of Education has the power to terminate on reasons given. . . .[29]

Although separation from the service seems to have been recommended in this instance, the usual procedure is to transfer unsatisfactory teachers; those who give evidence of physical or mental unfitness are referred to the head of the Child Guidance Bureau, who attempts to dissuade them from further professional work in the Chicago schools (*supra*[26]). But teachers who are given such advice are not obligated to take it.[30]

New Jersey

During the six-year period 1926-1931, the Committee on Grievances and Redress of the New Jersey State Teachers' Association

---

[27] Board Proceedings, Chicago, Ill., Feb. 9, 1927, p. 1172.
[28] Board Proceedings, Chicago, Ill., May 25, 1927, pp. 1586-588.
[29] Board Proceedings, Chicago, Ill., Oct. 14, 1925, p. 265.
[30] Board Proceedings, Chicago, Ill., Oct. 14, 1925, p. 265; Oct. 28, 1925, pp. 404-05; Jan. 13, 1926, p. 655.

gave advice on forty-six cases involving a total of sixty-six educational workers. It is probable that the total number of cases considered was considerably larger, for when a case is appealed to the State Department of Education the Committee ordinarily transmits all information it has pertaining thereto to the proper state official. Nine of the forty-six cases appearing in the records of the Committee were finally disposed of by state educational authorities and by the higher law courts; but during the six-year period in question approximately twenty cases were appealed to these authorities for judgment. Table XI shows the types of cases that came before the Committee and the respective numbers of each.

The type of case considered most frequently is that of the probationary teacher whose services are discontinued at the close of the three-year period of trial service. This device is commonly used by school boards in other indefinite tenure states for preventing teachers from gaining permanent status.

One case on which the Committee gave advice was that of five young unmarried teachers who had completed three years of school service, but not three calendar years, and who were refused new contracts. The local press was reported to have stated that the reason the board of education would not reëmploy the five teachers was that it opposed the Tenure of Office Law. Several such cases have been decided by state educational authorities and always against the teachers involved, except where three calendar years of service had been completed.

An interesting case of evasion of the law was that of a teacher who had served six school years in one position without gaining permanent status. The governing board forced the teacher to begin his fourth year of teaching two weeks late and thus break his continuity of service. This teacher was dropped at the end of his sixth year of service and there was no recourse to a higher authority open to him. As yet no test case has been had in New Jersey to determine how long a teacher must be out of the service to annul his accumulated tenure rights.

Discontinuance of services upon abolition of position ranks second in Table XI, eight such cases being listed. Local boards may eliminate positions made unnecessary by changes in organization or in the curriculum. Similarly, a change of district boundaries or the creation of a new district will cause teachers who are

TABLE XI

Types of Cases and Corresponding Numbers of Each Considered by the Committee on Grievances and Redress of the New Jersey State Teachers' Association from 1926–1931, Inclusive[1]

Type of Cases	Number of Cases	Number of Workers
1. Permanent status claimed by probationary employees		
a. Services discontinued end of third consecutive school year	10	12
b. Forced resignation to break continuity of service	1	1
2. Abolition of position		
a. Changes in organization or curriculum	4	6
b. School absorbed by newly-created district	1	1
c. For reasons of economy	1	1
d. No details	2	2
3. Alleged discrimination against married women		
a. Forced resignation	4	4
b. Salary increases denied	1	10
c. No details	1	1
4. Requests for advice	4	7
5. Unrequested and unwanted transfers		
a. To lower grade	2	5
b. To higher position	1	1
6. Dismissal for inefficiency, neglect of duty, insubordination, etc.	3	3
7. Dismissal for unbecoming personal conduct	2	2
8. Miscellaneous		
a. Absent without permission	2	2
b. Insufficient educational qualifications	2	2
c. Regular salary increases not granted	1	2
d. Salary suit based on claim of prohibition to teach for one year	1	1
e. No details	3	3
Total	46	66

[1] Data secured from the private records of the Committee on Grievances and Redress of the N. J. S. T. A.

thus placed under a new jurisdiction to lose the equities held in old positions. Bad faith was thought to exist in the case of the position abolished on grounds of economy, since a man was hired to take the place of the woman eliminated, but definite proof was lacking and the Committee did not feel that it could offer financial aid. One of the cases listed under "No details" was that of a supervising principal who claimed that she might have retained her position by paying $200. This individual was advised to watch developments and to fight the case if the position was recreated.

Alleged discrimination against married women teachers accounts for six of the cases in Table XI. One of the forced resignations under this head was caused by refusal of a local board to grant maternity leave; another was that of a newly-married teacher who resigned in compliance with a board rule, not knowing that the rule was unenforceable; and the other two were probationary teachers who were requested or compelled to break the continuity of their service so as to prevent accrual of permanent status. In all of these cases the Committee had to inform the interested parties that no remedy was available. Ten teachers were involved in the case of denial of regular salary increases, which was finally settled in favor of the teachers by the State Department of Education. Here the Committee recommended that should the case be further appealed, moral and financial support be afforded the teachers by the State Teachers' Association.

Two of the three cases of undesired transfer listed in Table XI were instances of transfer from the junior high school to the elementary school level. Appellants in these cases were informed that they had suffered no demotion in law, as no distinction is made among teachers, and that boards of education may transfer teachers as long as they do not reduce salaries. The case of transfer to a higher position was plainly a subterfuge on the part of the local board to replace a woman supervising principal with a man. A new position, that of director of research, was created and the woman promoted to it on probation at a higher salary than she had been receiving. She accepted under protest and immediately began to fight the case, aided by the Committee on Grievances and Redress. The following excerpt is from a letter of protest sent by the Committee to the local board of education:

> If this change endangers Miss ———'s right to tenure, we must very strongly protest this action in the name of the New Jersey State Teachers' Association composed of about thirty thousand members.

Termination of this dispute in favor of the "promoted" supervising principal was reported in the *Newark Evening News*:

> Miss ——— is again supervising principal of Cranford schools. In a stormy session of the Board of Education last night, as a result of which the president resigned office, the body rescinded its action of last month creating the position of director of research for the school system to which it then appointed Miss ———.
>
> Last night's action comes as a result of bitterly contended efforts to put a man in the supervising principal's position.[31]

Only one other type of case is worthy of specific comment, namely, that of the request for advice. One of the four cases listed under this head was that of an administrator who wished information with respect to his legal rights in a pending investigation of his administration. Another case concerned four teachers in a city system who wished to know whether their superintendent could demand that they give demonstration lessons. The other two were, respectively, a request for information regarding contract rights and an appeal for advice concerning tenure status. Much of the work of the Committee consists of giving advice and making recommendations, but usually after difficulties have arisen. It is only in cases of the kind described in this paragraph that the Committee has an opportunity to forestall unfortunate developments.

Up to the present time the Committee has not had the benefit of a consulting lawyer, although it has felt for some time that one is needed. The attitude of the Committee with regard to this point is shown by the following excerpts from the minutes:

> Mr. Kraybill made a motion that this committee recommend to the Executive Committee that it retain a lawyer for us to consult when necessary. Motion carried.[32]
>
> At each meeting the need of a lawyer for consultation is brought home to us in increasing intensity.[33]

Recommendation has also gone forward from the Committee to the Executive Committee of the Teachers' Association to the effect that the law be amended, if possible, requiring that school boards gain the consent of the Commissioner of Education before abolishing any positions (*supra*[32]).

The work of the New Jersey Committee on Grievances and Redress is duplicated in part in other states having indefinite tenure statutes; e.g., the California Teachers' Association has a legal advisor who assists with tenure cases and also a standing tenure

---

[31] *Newark Evening News*, about May 12, 1931. (Exact date unknown.)
[32] Minutes of the Committee on Grievances and Redress, N.J.S.T.A., Nov. 10, 1930.
[33] *Ibid.*, May 1, 1931.

committee; and other state associations have tenure committees that study problems and assist teachers whose tenure rights are jeopardized. It also has its counterpart in at least one foreign country. In England and Wales the National Union of Teachers through its Tenure Committee plays a most important rôle in enforcing the tenure rights of teachers in the public schools.

SUMMARY

This chapter has demonstrated, through the use of published comments on indefinite tenure and data taken from former research studies and from case studies made by the writer, the most popular claims made for indefinite tenure and the fallacies thereof as well as the major operative effects. Published comments were taken from local and national educational journals and are valuable largely for their exposition of unfounded claims and of real tenure problems; they vary somewhat in viewpoint and in no case have the authority of scientific investigation. Data from previous research studies and the writer's investigations are admittedly limited, but are sufficient for identification of problems and for all conclusions drawn. Two-thirds of the principal claims made for indefinite tenure are untenable and these, along with the valid one-third, constitute either singly or together serious problems. These problems, like all others treated in this chapter, belong in some cases peculiarly to the field of indefinite tenure and in others to the whole field of teacher personnel. Results of the writer's study are forthwith briefly epitomized.

1. Undoubtedly the biggest problem arising under indefinite tenure laws is that of removing undesirable teachers from office. In some large cities, e.g., Duluth, Minneapolis, and Saint Paul, Minnesota, and Newark, New Jersey, whole years pass without the dismissal of a single teacher. Difficulty of removal may vary among the states, but it exists in all that have protective tenure statutes.

2. Correlatively, teachers in all or practically all indefinite tenure states enjoy a high degree of protection from unprofessional attacks and from anxiety regarding the safety of their positions. One of the weakest state laws in this respect is that of Massachusetts.

3. Indefinite tenure may tend to stabilize the profession, to in-

crease its drawing power, and to increase the interest of teachers in professional improvement, yet proof to this effect has still to be produced. Measurement of such possible results of indefinite tenure will always be difficult owing to the operation of a number of other important factors.

4. Fixed probationary periods, of the type now universally in force, seem to impose a burden upon some teachers, since local boards rather commonly drop probationers to prevent their gaining permanent status. It is also probable that trial periods serve no useful purpose from a training standpoint, but merely afford a chance for officials to judge a teacher.

5. Rural teachers are known to be a special problem in two of the five states where such teachers have protection, i.e., California and Indiana. Because of this, ostensibly, the 1931 California law makes indefinite tenure optional in districts with less than 850 A.D.A.

6. Unsatisfactory teachers are somewhat frequently given transfers or requested to resign, thus making unnecessary outright dismissal.

7. The laws of the District of Columbia, Colorado, Indiana, Minnesota, and New Jersey offer either potential or actual obstacles to changes in salary policies, i.e., to reductions. Retirement and tenure regulations are naturally closely related, as was shown by the unsuccessful attempt of the Chicago Board of Education to retire superannuated teachers.

8. Miscellaneous problems that seem to be either local or general are the married woman teacher, restricted application and indefinite wording of some laws, and the tendency of some administrative officials to evade the provisions and express intent of the laws.

9. Detailed facts concerning tenure and related cases arising under the Illinois and New Jersey laws serve mainly to illustrate the several problems and to show the types of cases that arise. Variations of unsatisfactory service and insubordination account for a majority of the Chicago cases and for a very small number of the New Jersey cases. Non-retention of probationary teachers, abolition of position, alleged discrimination against married women teachers, and requests for advice, in the order named, have been considered most frequently by the Committee on Grievances and Redress of the New Jersey State Teachers' Association.

Operation of Tenure Laws

10. The Committee just mentioned performs a valuable service for New Jersey teachers, both by giving advice on questions of tenure and by securing financial aid for the prosecution of tenure cases when the conditions warrant. Similar work is carried on by other state teachers' associations in the United States and also by the National Union of Teachers of England and Wales.

SELECTED REFERENCES

CHICAGO BOARD OF EDUCATION. *Proceedings of the Board of Education,* 1920-1931. Chicago, Ill.

DIX, LESTER. "The Educational Personnel of the Schools." *Report of the Survey of the Schools of Chicago, Illinois,* Vol. I, pp. 290-97. Division of Field Studies, Institute of Educational Research. Bureau of Publications, Teachers College, Columbia University, New York, 1932.

DODGE, H. S. "Desirable Changes in the Teacher Tenure Law." *Bulletin of the Associated School Boards and Trustees of the State of New York,* 3:7-9, June 1931.

EDITORIAL. "Removal for Cause." *Common Ground,* 2:136, October 1922.

EDITORIAL. "Rural Schools and Tenure." *Indiana Teacher,* 73:16, January 1929.

EDITORIAL. "Two Observations on Teacher Tenure." *Indiana Teacher,* 76:18, October 1931.

NEW JERSEY STATE TEACHERS' ASSOCIATION. *Records of the Committee on Grievances and Redress,* 1926-1931. (Private records kept by the Secretary of the Committee.)

CHAPTER V

Operation of Existing State Indefinite Teacher Tenure Laws as Revealed by Appeal Cases

RECORDS of appeal cases in which real or alleged indefinite tenure rights were violated by the actions of local boards afford excellent material for studying the operation of and for critically evaluating the statutes involved. In fact, data obtained from this source are perhaps the most reliable that can be secured on the question of the effects of indefinite teacher tenure laws. Changes in rates of turnover, in amounts of professional preparation and in-service training, and in the type of individuals entering the teaching profession—all of which have been used in judging protective tenure—are unquestionably the products of a number of factors. But appeal cases arise solely from tenure disputes and the decisions thereon and are distinctly revelatory concerning the operation of existing laws.

This chapter presents a comprehensive treatment of all appeal cases decided by higher educational and legal tribunals from the respective dates of passage of the several state laws through 1931. Not all of these cases resulted from dismissals, but a majority of them did. The chief value of the chapter is that it shows how indefinite tenure laws have been interpreted and applied by appeal authorities. Other values are that it reveals, at least by implication, good and bad features of the statutes and presents statistical or summary facts regarding the appeal cases.

COMPOSITE DATA

Table XII, which lists all appeal cases through 1931 according to type, final ruling authority, and decisions handed down, gives the total for the twelve states and the District of Columbia as 137. Of this number, eighty-five, or 62.04 per cent, were decided in favor of the contesting boards and fifty-two, or 37.96 per cent, in favor of aggrieved teachers. The trend of decisions indicates that

Tenure Laws as Revealed by Appeal Cases

TABLE XII
APPEAL CASES WITH DECISIONS THEREON THAT HAVE ARISEN UNDER THE SEVERAL STATE INDEFINITE TEACHER TENURE LAWS FROM THE DATES OF PASSAGE THROUGH 1931[1]

Type of Cases	Final Authority				Decisions		
	Commissioner of Education	State Board	Supreme Court	Appellate Court	Favoring Teacher	Favoring Board	Total
1. Various combinations of the following charges, each including two or more: Inefficiency, incompetency, unprofessional and unbecoming conduct, insubordination, and refusal to cooperate	12	8	3	1	8	16	24
2. Summary dismissal	3	3	4	7	13	4	17
3. Non-retention of probationary teachers	8	3	2	4	1	16	17
4. Abolition of position	9	2	3	0	3	11	14
5. Transfers involving demotions in rank and salary or in rank only; also those producing no change in status	7	2	4	0	6	7	13
6. Women teachers dismissed upon marriage	0	2	4	2	7	1	8
7. Reduction of salary	1	3	2	1	2	5	7
8. Conduct unbecoming of a teacher	3	2	0	0	2	3	5
9. Suits by reinstated teachers for salary losses during periods of suspension	1	0	2	1	2	2	4
10. Insubordination	0	2	1	0	0	3	3
11. Certification questions	1	1	0	1	1	2	3
12. Tenure protection claimed by permanently ineligible school employees	1	0	2	0	0	3	3
13. Miscellaneous, e.g., resignation questions, forced leaves of absence, suspensions—illegal and otherwise, etc. (No more than two cases of any one type.)	7	5	4	3	7	12	19
Total	53	33	31	20	52	85	137

[1] Data obtained from annual reports of state departments of education and from decisions of courts of record.

local boards of education have a real advantage in appeal cases; but it could hardly be termed great enough to cause them to abuse their powers. This advantage is no doubt ascribable to the tendency on the part of appeal authorities to respect the findings of local boards.

That the trend of decisions is the same regardless of the final deciding authority is clearly shown by Table XIII. The handicap for teachers is about constant for three of the four authorities, but decreases appreciably in the case of the Supreme Court. These data, with those of Table XIV, seem to invalidate, at least in part, the old claim that protective tenure laws make virtually impossible the removal of undesirable teachers who have gained permanent status, particularly if appeal to regular law courts is allowed.

TABLE XIII

Distribution of Appeal Cases Arising under State Indefinite Teacher Tenure Laws According to Final Ruling Authority and Decisions Rendered[1]

Final Authority	Number of Decisions Favoring Board	Number of Decisions Favoring Teacher
Commissioner of Education	33	20
State Board of Education	22	12
Supreme Court	17	13
Appellate Court	13	7
Total	85	52

[1] This distribution contains all cases decided by state departments of education and courts of record through 1931.

According to Table XIV, the right of appeal in tenure cases has but little significance in Massachusetts and New York, while California and New Jersey teachers have a fairly good chance of winning appeals. The figures for Massachusetts corroborate a statement made in Chapter IV to the effect that the indefinite tenure law of this state affords a relatively small degree of protection for teachers. And again, the figures given for the Commissioner of Education in New Jersey and in New York reveal a difference in trends which must be credited either to unlike attitudes toward questions of tenure on the part of these officials or to differences in the laws of the two states. A comparison of Supreme Court decisions for New Jersey and New York reveals similar results, explainable in the same way. Variations in decisions

Tenure Laws as Revealed by Appeal Cases

due to each of the two causes mentioned will receive further attention in other sections of this chapter.

TABLE XIV

DISTRIBUTION OF INDEFINITE TEACHER TENURE APPEAL CASES FOR CALIFORNIA, MASSACHUSETTS, NEW JERSEY, AND NEW YORK ACCORDING TO FINAL RULING AUTHORITY AND DECISIONS RENDERED[1]

Final Authority	California		Massachusetts		New Jersey		New York	
	Favoring Board	Favoring Teacher	Favoring Board	Favoring Teacher	Favoring Board	Favoring Teacher	Favoring Board	Favoring Teacher
Commissioner of Education	0	0	0	0	17	15	16	5
State Board of Education	0	0	0	0	22	11	0	0
Supreme Court ..	0	2	7	2	3	4	3	0
Appellate Court .	8	5	0	0	1	0	2	0
Total	8	7	7	2	43	30	21	5

[1] This distribution contains all cases decided through 1931 by the respective state departments of education and by courts of record in the four states.

The chronological distribution of appeal cases presented in Table XV shows that the rate of occurrence is rather uniform in states where a considerable number have arisen. These numerical facts bear out the claim already made that the advantage local boards have in appeal cases is not sufficient to cause them to abuse their authority or to intimidate teachers.

Discussion of the nature of appeal cases and presentation of material therefrom are reserved for the remainder of this chapter. Suffice it to note here that the general charges of inefficiency, unprofessional and unbecoming conduct, and insubordination have occurred more commonly than any others; that dismissal without notice and dropping of probationary teachers jointly rank second in frequency; and that abolition of position and transfers of different type hold the third and fourth ranks, respectively. Dismissal of women teachers upon marriage and reduction of salary disputes, in the fifth and sixth ranks, are also worthy of mention. Each of the other types appearing in Table XII accounts for only a small number of cases, except for the miscellaneous group, which is really second in point of size. This group, however, has no more than two cases of any one kind.

Indefinite Teacher Tenure

TABLE XV

Chronological Distribution of Appeal Cases Arising under the Several State Indefinite Teacher Tenure Laws from the Respective Dates of Passage Through 1931[1]

Date of Final Decision	Number of Cases in Each State										
	Cal.	Col.	D. C.	Ill.	Md.	Mass.	Minn.	N. J.	N. Y.	Ore.	Wis.
1906	--	--	1	--	--	--	--	--	--	--	--
1908	--	--	1	--	--	--	--	--	--	--	--
1911	--	--	--	--	--	--	--	1	--	--	--
1912	--	--	--	--	--	--	--	5	--	--	--
1913	--	--	--	--	--	--	--	3	--	--	--
1914	--	--	--	--	--	--	--	8	--	--	--
1915	--	--	--	--	--	--	--	3	--	1	--
1916	--	--	1	--	--	--	--	3	--	--	--
1917	--	--	--	--	--	--	--	3	--	1	--
1918	--	--	--	--	--	--	--	3	3	--	--
1919	--	--	--	--	--	--	--	1	3	--	--
1920	--	--	--	--	--	1	--	1	--	1	--
1921	--	--	1	--	--	--	--	2	4	--	--
1922	--	--	--	--	--	--	--	3	--	--	--
1923	1	--	--	--	--	--	--	5	1	--	1
1924	3	--	--	--	--	3	--	3	2	--	--
1925	--	--	--	--	--	--	--	4	1	--	--
1926	--	--	--	--	--	--	--	5	4	--	1
1927	2	--	--	--	--	--	--	3	1	--	--
1928	1	1	--	1	--	--	--	4	2	--	--
1929	3	--	--	--	--	--	1	5	1	1	--
1930	2	--	--	--	--	1	--	3	2	--	--
1931	3	--	--	--	1	4	--	5	2	--	--
Total	15	1	4	1	1	9	1	73	26	4	2

[1] All appeal cases decided by higher educational and legal tribunals are included in this table. No cases occurred during the years or in the states omitted.

CONSTITUTIONALITY OF INDEFINITE TENURE LAWS

Wherever the constitutionality of state indefinite teacher tenure laws has been questioned, final decisions have always asserted the right of states thus to protect their public school teachers. Attacks on the laws have without exception been based either on the claim that these statutes are discriminatory, since they classify school districts or teachers, or both, or on the assumption that they violate contractual rights. Both of these charges were made against the original California law in the famous case of Grigsby v. King[1] and both set aside by the Supreme Court in its reversal

[1] Grigsby v. King et al., 74 Cal. Dec. 439 (1927).

of the trial court. The discrimination plea was here based on the fact that the law did not apply in small districts, i.e., in those having less than eight teachers and no regular supervisory service. This provision of the law was defended by the Court on the ground that boards of trustees in small districts, not having the benefit of expert educational counsel, cannot reasonably determine the propriety of according a teacher permanent status within a definite period of time. Furthermore, the Court held that there is just as much reason for classifying school districts as for classifying cities, and also that, in the last analysis, the classification was based upon population and was therefore not unjust. With regard to the contention concerning contractual rights, the Court held that the provisions of the State Constitution relative to personal rights are inapplicable to

> an impersonal, administrative agency such as a board of school trustees exercising special and limited powers and having no existence except by legal enactment. . . . (*supra*[1])

The discrimination charge has also been leveled unsuccessfully at the Wisconsin law, which applies only to Milwaukee.[2]

While recognizing that determination of the constitutionality of legislation is a province of the courts, the State Board of Education of New Jersey has twice ruled that, in the absence of court decisions, the Teachers' Tenure of Service Act is not in violation of the provisions of the State Constitution prohibiting the enactment of laws violating the obligations of contracts.[3, 4]

PURPOSE, OR THEORY, UNDERLYING INDEFINITE TENURE LAWS

Protection of teachers in their positions and safeguarding the rights of school children are the reasons given for indefinite tenure laws by state educational authorities and the law courts. In a California decision, the Appellate Court stated the purpose of the ruling protective tenure law thus:

> It seems to us apparent . . . that the legislative intent is manifest to give assurance to the teaching profession of some degree of certainty in their employment . . . something akin to civil service in other administrative branches of government.[5]

---

[2] Nyberg v. Milwaukee, 209 N. W. 683 (1926).
[3] Clayton v. Orange, N. J. S. R., Vol. 1, 1913, 233.
[4] Marstellar v. Pleasantville, N. J. S. R., 1912, 104.
[5] Blalock v. Ridgway et al., 92 Cal. App. 132 (1928).

But a dissenting opinion rendered in this case gives the intent of the law as follows:

> It is unthinkable that the legislature should intend to enact any provision which would make the financial interests of a teacher paramount to the best interests, welfare and proper education of the school children. The whole system of legislation regulating the educational machinery was based upon consideration of the welfare and best interests of the children as the original and fundamental purposes. (*supra*[5])

Similarly, a Commissioner of Education in New York recently upheld the rights of the child as the fundamental interest which the state seeks to protect.

> This provision of law [subd. 3, sec. 872] was enacted for the primary purpose of providing the schools with efficient and suitable teachers and of guaranteeing, so far as may be possible, to the children . . . their right to receive instruction from competent, experienced and proper teachers. The theory is that permanent tenure will attract men and women of the best intellectual attainments to the teaching service; that teachers will make more thorough academic and professional preparation, will remain in the service longer and thus bring to the support of the schools teachers whose training and experience will be a valuable asset.[6]

A later decision, however, made by another Commissioner, holds that the indefinite tenure law is clearly for the benefit of teachers, while admitting that, at least theoretically, it is of benefit to an entire school system.[7] The Supreme Court of New York recently held that the transparent purpose of the law is to protect teachers and other educational employees.[8]

Teacher protection appears to be the main object of the Wisconsin law, according to a Supreme Court decision (*supra*[2]). No expression of the purpose of the tenure regulations operating in the District of Columbia appears in any appeal cases arising thereunder, still the Appellate Court of the District has stated that the tenor of educational legislation by Congress looks toward permanency in the teaching force and that the welfare of the schools demands such a policy.[9]

As in the case of California and New York, dissenting opinions have been voiced concerning the *raison d'être* of the New Jersey law. On one hand the State Board of Education has held that the

---

[6] Matter of Appeal of Mufson, Schneer, and Schmalhausen, 18 N.Y.S.D.R. 393 (1918).
[7] Matter of Appeal of Boyd, 40 N. Y. S. D. R. 248 (1931).
[8] Holm v. Rochester, 252 N. Y. S. 389 (1931).
[9] District of Columbia v. Dean, 38 App. D. C. 182 (1912).

purpose of the statute is to protect principals and teachers in their positions;[10] and on the other the Attorney General has declared that, to his mind, the aim of the State Legislature was "expression of a public policy for the benefit of the school system."[11] Finally, Leech[12] is authority for the statement that the courts of New Jersey have ruled that the indefinite tenure law of the state was enacted, "not for the especial benefit of employees, but for the improvement of the service and of the standards of the public school system."

ELIGIBILITY REQUIREMENTS FOR TENURE PROTECTION

Decisions in appeal cases have established three prerequisites for protection under indefinite tenure laws: (1) classification as an employee to whom protection is available; (2) completion of a prescribed probationary period; and (3) possession of the type of certificate required for the work being done. Appeal authorities in Massachusetts,[13] New Jersey,[14] and New York[15] have held that employees of boards of education in positions upon which tenure protection has not been conferred by school law, either directly or at the option of employing boards, have no valid claim to indefinite tenure rights. A good illustrative case is that of Lamarsh v. Chicopee (*supra*[13]), in which a dismissed clerical worker with the title of "assistant to principal" unsuccessfully claimed tenure protection. Substitute teachers ordinarily cannot gain permanent status; but in New Jersey substitutes under full-time employment acquire tenure protection upon completing the regular probationary period.[16] That teachers must be employed in districts where tenure laws apply, provided they are not state-wide in application, in order to enjoy tenure security has been decided by the higher courts of Colorado[17] and New York.[18]

The requirement of completion of a legally prescribed period of test service for indefinite tenure protection has been upheld

[10] Pearce et al. *v.* Gloucester City. In Ms. (1923).
[11] *Ed. Bul.* (N. J.), Vol. 11, No. 2, p. 47, Oct. 1924.
[12] Leech, Carl G., *The Constitutional and Legal Basis of Education in New Jersey*, p. 350.
[13] Lamarsh *v.* Chicopee, 172 N. E. 117 (1930).
[14] Mobins and Ghesquier *v.* Paterson, N. J. S. R., 1925, 445.
[15] Matter of Appeal of Sweeney, 35 N. Y. S. D. R. 573 (1926).
[16] Waters *v.* Newark. In Ms. (1931).
[17] Ryan *v.* Sch. Dist. No. 26, Arapahoe Co., 270 P. 865 (1928).
[18] Chase *v.* Mason, 216 N. Y. S. 205.

by decisions rendered in New Jersey[19, 20] and New York.[21, 22] Practically all such cases have arisen from misinterpretation by teachers of the governing laws.

As for the necessity of a teacher's being properly certificated, Allen[23] has pointed out that an uncertificated teacher cannot teach a legal school. Naturally, this holds for teachers serving under protective tenure laws as well as for those on yearly contracts. A case in point is that of McAuley v. Prospect Park,[24] in which the New Jersey State Board ruled:

> It was her affair, her business to see to it that she had a certificate. Not having it she was not under the tenure of service act, and the Board of Education was not only justified in dismissing her in January, 1914, but should not have employed her or paid her after the expiration of her second grade county teacher's certificate in June, 1913. From that time on she was not entitled to teach in the public schools of New Jersey.[24]

Modern developments in teacher certification have made it necessary for educational workers to hold special types of certificates qualifying them for particular kinds of work. However, teachers with permanent status enjoy a distinct advantage here, since they may demand that they be assigned the type of work for which they are certificated.[25]

LEGAL INTERPRETATION OF MAJOR PROTECTIONS AFFORDED TEACHERS

The most important protective features of indefinite tenure laws from the standpoint of teachers with permanent status are that dismissals are possible only after charges have been filed in a fixed manner and an orderly hearing held, and that any dismissed teacher is privileged to appeal her case to a higher educational or legal authority, perhaps to both such authorities, for a final decision.[26]

[19] Brandes v. Hoboken, N. J. S. L. D., 1921, 550 (1913).
[20] Carrol v. St. Bd. of Ed., 8 N. J. M. R. 859 (1930).
[21] Matter of Appeal of Crum, MacLellan, Pratt, Sill, and Taylor, 20 N. Y. S. D. R. 195 (1919).
[22] Matter of Appeal of Mandigo, 35 N. Y. S. D. R. 633 (1926).
[23] Allen, Ira M., *The Teacher's Contractual Status*, pp. 14-15.
[24] McAuley v. Prospect Park, N. J. S. R., 1916, 189.
[25] Bagnell v. Bayonne, N. J. S. R., 1915, 61.
[26] In all states having indefinite tenure laws without appeal provisions, the right of a dismissed teacher to appeal to courts of law is recognized by other sections of the school codes or by common law.

Summary Dismissal

Seventeen cases of summary dismissal have come before appeal authorities, as shown in Table XII, and in thirteen of these decisions have been rendered for the appellant teachers. Such verdicts invariably assert that contracts of permanent teachers are terminable only according to prescribed legal procedures. The four decisions in favor of defendant boards turned on the following points: (1) failure to show eligibility for protection;[27] (2) lack of definiteness of law concerning its application as to employees;[28] (3) dilatoriness of appellant in beginning appeal action;[29] and (4) the claim of the Board of Education of the District of Columbia that it is not estopped by any existing law from inquiring into the professional qualifications of teachers and then taking such action as may appear best for the good of the service.[30]

Manner of Preferring Charges and Nature Thereof

With the exceptions just noted, decisions in cases of summary dismissal have upheld the right of permanent teachers to have formal charges preferred against them before being dismissed; but the manner in which charges should be preferred has been commented on in only a few decisions of one state, New Jersey. The right of a pupil to enter charges against a teacher was established in Smith v. Phillipsburg;[31] and in the case of Davis v. Overpeck[32] the State Board ruled that "any citizen may file charges against a teacher with the local school board." Reluctance on the part of a board to bring charges of inefficiency cannot be used to estop the board or the public from such action.[33] Charges must be in writing, according to the decision in Pearce et al. v. Gloucester City (supra[10]).

In a Massachusetts decision,[34] where the nature of charges was an issue, it was held that the School Committee could not be forced to give detailed reasons for a proposed dismissal, although a statement of reasons is required by law if requested by the teacher. In its concluding comment on this case, the court said:

[27] Clark v. Eureka School Dist. et al., 64 Cal. App. 757 (1923).
[28] Bland v. Galt Joint Union H. S. Dist. et al., 67 Cal. App. 784 (1924).
[29] Barhite v. West New York, 86 N. J. L. 674 (1914).
[30] U. S. ex rel. Nalle v. Hoover, 31 App. D. C. 311 (1908).
[31] Smith v. Phillipsburg, N. J. S. R., 1917, 313.
[32] Davis v. Overpeck Twp., N. J. S. R., 1916, 209.
[33] Conrow v. Lumberton Twp., 1 N. J. S. R., 1913, 231.
[34] Corrigan v. New Bedford, 250 Mass. 334 (1924).

The right of the school committee to engage a teacher at their discretion would be largely abrogated if the construction of the statute contended for by the petitioner were adopted [detailed specification of charges]. (*supra*[34])

The New Jersey State Board of Education has held with regard to a claim of insufficient charges that

... the charges were sufficient if Mr. ——— was by them so apprised of the complaints against him, that he understood their nature, and could, if he so desired, prepare to meet them.[35]

A contract case[36] that occurred in New York sets forth a viewpoint similar to that expressed by the New Jersey State Board. In this case the court held that dismissal charges against a teacher should not be ambiguous or general, but should be directed to specific acts in order that the accused may know with what she is charged and thus be prepared to defend herself.

Hearing Requirement and Its Nature

Special comment on the necessity of an orderly hearing, to which all permanent teachers are entitled before dismissal, has appeared in two New York cases[37, 38] and in one New Jersey case (*supra*[10]). With regard to the privilege of New York teachers to a hearing before dismissal and the nature of such, an acting Commissioner recently said:

This provision [the indefinite tenure statute] does not deprive boards of education of their discretionary power to remove or suspend teachers who have served the probationary period, but limits the exercise of such discretion to cases where cause for dismissal is shown to exist after a hearing. The statute does not prescribe the procedure but the requirement of a hearing implies that there shall be charges, notice and opportunity to defend. The courts have repeatedly held that under such a statute formal and technical rules of evidence do not control, and that all of the formalities of a trial before a judicial tribunal need not be observed.[38]

The other two cases cited merely refer to the respective hearing provisions of the two state laws and affirm their right to operate in all dismissal cases.

According to a California decision,[39] a local board may treat as a nullity an attempt at summary dismissal and proceed with a trial

[35] Fitch *v.* South Amboy, N. J. S. L. D., 1928, 173 (1914).
[36] Morton *v.* Weet, 254 N. Y. S. 655 (1931).
[37] Matter of Appeal of Healy, 34 N. Y. S. D. R. 449 (1926).
[38] Matter of Appeal of Shea and Foody, 26 N. Y. S. D. R. 469 (1921).
[39] Alexander *v.* Manton Joint Union Sch. Dist., 73 Cal. App. 252 (1927).

Tenure Laws as Revealed by Appeal Cases

of the teacher in question on charges. An unusual holding in this case was that an unaccepted offer of the trustees to submit proof of their charges at the original hearing was sufficient. Ordinarily, all dismissal cases are heard by the ruling boards of education; but it has been held that the Committee on High Schools and Training Schools of New York City has the power to hear cases (*supra*[6]). This decision was based on Section 1093 of the city charter.

Since evidence produced in hearings before local boards is generally used by higher tribunals when cases are appealed, it would appear that stenographic records should be kept of all original hearings. However, this is not a universal practice among indefinite tenure states and the matter has figured in but one appeal case.[40] New Jersey authorities once held that a stenographic record must be taken of the testimony in a hearing (*supra*[40]); but a late decision in a janitor tenure case[41] avers that a record of this type cannot be required in the absence of a statute prescribing it. In at least one New Jersey case, the incompleteness of the minutes of an original hearing made it necessary for the Commissioner on appeal of the case, to take testimony *de novo*.[42]

Appeal Rights and Procedures

As has already been stated (page 78) permanent teachers whose tenure rights are violated may appeal their cases to higher educational or legal authorities, or to both. In a few states, for instance, Massachusetts and Wisconsin, appeals must be taken directly from the decisions of local boards to the courts; while in others, for example, New Jersey and New York, every effort is made to keep appeal cases out of the courts. Remarks of appeal authorities with regard to the subject at hand cover largely questions of the right to appeal, the manner of making appeals, the power of ruling authorities, and the bases for decisions.

The California case of Alexander *v.* Manton (*supra*[39]), affirms the prerogative of dismissed permanent teachers in that state to enter suit in a court to determine the truth or falsity of charges filed against them. In another case arising in the same state, the Supreme Court pointed out that the courts have frequently held

---

[40] White *v.* Readington, N. J. S. R., 1927, 87.
[41] Follmer *v.* Jersey City, N. J. S. R., 1928, 78.
[42] Wallace *v.* Greenwich Twp. In Ms. (1931).

that mandamus is the proper remedy to be invoked by a teacher wrongfully dismissed who holds a position "not under contract but by virtue of statutory authority."[43] Similar decisions in other states have universally upheld the privilege of permanent teachers to appeal.

Teachers in New York ordinarily are required to carry their complaints from the decisions of local boards to the Commissioner of Education, whose pronouncements are final. In McDowell v. New York City,[44] a teacher who was dismissed for pacifism during the World War was instructed by the Supreme Court that her only recourse was an appeal to the Commissioner. Equivalent decisions have been handed down by the courts in two other cases.[45, 46] The power of the Commissioner to hear and decide appeal cases has been set forth as follows:

> We therefore conclude that as to all matters appealable to the Commissioner of Education under section 890 of the Education Law, he has exclusive jurisdiction; such conclusion is supported by the authorities and by the obvious purpose of the Education Law.[45]

Reasons for according the New York Commissioner complete authority in appeal cases appear in McDowell v. New York City (supra[44]), after a prefatory statement to the effect that the state has always regarded the maintenance of an effective education system as of vital importance to its welfare and has insisted upon supervising the training of its children.

> The plan of having such appeals referred to the Commissioner was advisedly and wisely adopted. By that means it was assured that all questions relating to the schools, of which the qualification of a teacher is not the least important, could be submitted to one whose experience is daily broadened in the administration of his duties as Commissioner of Education and whose power fully to investigate the circumstances is unrestricted.[44]

There seems to be no doubt as to the finality of decisions made by the New York Commissioner; but a question does exist as to whether under certain conditions a case may not be appealed either to the Commissioner or to the courts. Although it has been held by the Court of Appeals (supra[46]), that the necessity of construing a statute does not deprive the Commissioner of

---

[43] Saxton v. Los Angeles et al., 77 Cal. Dec. 493 (1929).
[44] McDowell v. New York City, 104 N. Y. M. R. 564 (1918).
[45] Bronson v. Binghamton, 136 N. Y. M. R. 76 (1930).
[46] Levitch v. New York City, 209 N. Y. S. 271, 243 N. Y. 373 (1926).

Tenure Laws as Revealed by Appeal Cases 83

jurisdiction, it has also been held by the Appellate Division of the Supreme Court that in such a case the courts likewise have jurisdiction to decide the matter.[47] And in a more recent case decided by the Supreme Court it was stated that whether or not the teacher's sole resort was to the Commissioner, assuming equal access to the courts the application failed (*supra*[8]).

The two cases just cited indicate that under certain circumstances the courts of New York may accept and rule on appeal cases; but they do not disprove the claim that the purpose of the Education Law of the state is to remove all matters pertaining to public education as far as practicable and possible from controversies in the courts. This statement is borne out by the two quotations above and is also admirably stated in the non-tenure case of Bullock *v.* Cooley.[48]

Information regarding the matter of authorities to whom appeals lie is given in only one other case, namely, the New Jersey controversy of Pearce et al. *v.* Gloucester City (*supra*[10]), in which it was definitely implied that cases should go first to the Commissioner of Education and then to the State Board. Except for New York and possibly Maryland, the last resort of teachers in indefinite tenure disputes is the regular courts of law.

All appeal cases on record have originated with either the teachers or local boards concerned, but for two exceptions (*supra*[10, 32]). In each of these a group of citizens tried to start an appeal with the result that their action was declared invalid. The State Board held in Davis *v.* Overpeck Township (*supra*[32]), that if citizens are dissatisfied with the rulings of public officials their only recourse is to the courts through certiorari proceedings.

But few precedents have been established by appeal cases with regard to the time within which appeal action must be started after local boards have rendered decisions. The Appellate Court of California has held that delay by an ousted permanent teacher until a new one was hired was no estoppal of appeal action.[49] But a three years' delay by a supervising principal in New Jersey was termed laches, or negligence, invalidating any tenure rights the appellant might have had at the time of dismissal (*supra*[29]).

The matter could have been decided in three months, and the appellant should have pushed his claim to a decision. The consequences of his not

[47] O'Connor *v.* Emerson et al., 188 N. Y. S. 236 (1921).
[48] Bullock *v.* Cooley, 225 N. Y. 566.
[49] Anderson *v.* Scranton et al., 295 P. 544 (1931).

doing so should fall upon his own head rather than upon the head of the Board of Education of West New York. (*supra*[29])

"Laches" has been defined by the California Appellate Court as not mere delay, but delay with changed conditions "from which injury would result to adverse party, or from which injury necessarily must be presumed."[50]

Appeal authorities ordinarily use as a basis for their decisions the evidence presented before local boards in hearings and used by them in arriving at the original verdicts. This is always the case with educational officers or bodies and likewise holds to a high degree with the law courts. In the New Jersey case of White v. Readington (*supra*[40]), the Commissioner stated that the only way for him to evaluate the decision of a local board was by review of facts produced before said body and then outlined his rôle thus:

> The function of the Commissioner in such case is not therefore to hear de novo the charges against the appellant, but to review and consider the legal sufficiency of the facts already before the local board of education and upon which it reached its conclusion.[40]

The State Board of Education of New Jersey has clearly indicated in several decisions that its policy in appeal cases is to respect the honest judgment of local boards. In Gebhart v. Hopewell,[51] this body answered the claim that the decision of the local board was not justified by the evidence with the following statement:

> This board has repeatedly held that in the absence of a showing of passion or prejudice, the determination of a district board on a question of this kind will not be disturbed unless the record contains no evidence to support it. If there are reasonable grounds to sustain the decision, it will not be reversed. (Ayres v. Newark, 20 Vroome 170; Ackerly v. Jersey City, 54 N.J.L. 311).[51]

Even in a case where incompleteness of the minutes of the proceedings at the original hearing made it necessary for the Commissioner to take testimony *de novo*, the State Board ruled that the issue was not to determine whether the evidence sustained the charges, but rather to find whether or not an illegal and improper dismissal had taken place (*supra*[42]).

That the New York Commissioner customarily relies upon the

---
[50] LaShells v. Hench et al., 276 P. 377 (1929).
[51] Gebhart v. Hopewell, N. J. S. R., 1928, 48.

facts presented in local hearings is clearly implied in McDowell *v.* New York City (*supra*[44]), in which the statement is made that he does not have to rely on such testimony, but may direct the district superintendent in any district where a dispute arises to take and report to him the evidence in the case. If the district superintendent needs to subpœna witnesses in carrying out such a request, he has the privilege of so doing.

Decisions handed down by higher courts of law are naturally based on evidence adduced in hearings before lower tribunals. In New Jersey only higher courts can receive appeal cases and in New York all courts generally refuse to rule on indefinite tenure cases. Lower courts receive cases only in states where no provision is made for appeal by aggrieved teachers to educational authorities, e.g., Indiana and Massachusetts. Evidence is lacking regarding the nature of trials in these courts save for California, in which state lower courts commonly received appeals prior to the passage of the 1931 indefinite tenure law. The Supreme Court of California ruled in Saxton *v.* Los Angeles (*supra*[43]), a case received on appeal from a county superior court, that the trial court had the power to determine the sufficiency and character of evidence in the case without hindrance by previous board action. Whether or not such authority works a hardship on local boards of education could be determined only by a study of decisions rendered by lower courts exercising this privilege.

POWER OF LOCAL BOARDS UNDER INDEFINITE TEACHER TENURE LAWS

Rights and powers of local boards of education in the administration of teacher personnel under protective tenure laws are limited particularly as regards the making and enforcement of rules and regulations and the dismissal of educational employees. The laws themselves, which local boards cannot ignore (*supra*[50]), prescribe procedures for the latter, and appeal authorities have held that rules and regulations which contravene the provisions of the laws are not enforceable.

No rule or by-law of a board of education which conflicts with the Teachers' Tenure of Service Act is enforceable. The board can, if it so desires, pass a rule or by-law concerning the effect of marriage and against absence without leave, but under the Tenure of Service Act, no teacher can be discharged unless charges are preferred against her, she is given a fair hearing to answer them, and it is found . . . that she is guilty. . . . The action of the Appellant in enforcing its rules and refusing Mrs. Nommensen a hearing was therefore contrary to the statute.[52]

Practically all cases centering around board rules and regulations have arisen from dismissal of women teachers upon marriage, and such cases have, with one exception,[53] been decided against the contesting boards.[54]

Although local boards are prohibited from dismissing permanent teachers except according to due processes of law, they are universally recognized as having the sole right to prosecute charges against teachers. This fact is well stated in the New Jersey case of Davis v. Overpeck (supra[32]). Another case from the same state, Gebhart v. Hopewell (supra[51]), settles the question of the propriety of board members acting as judges.

> It is said they [the board] are accusers rather than judges, and the plaintiff could not secure a fair and impartial hearing before them. Nevertheless these defendants constitute the only tribunal before which such hearing could be originally had. Code 2783.[51]

Massachusetts boards, or committees, are restricted in discharging teachers only in that, upon request, they must give a brief statement of charges and allow hearings (supra[34]). It is required that the superintendent's recommendation be given in each case, but committees are not obligated to accept same (supra[53]). In discussing the discretion which boards exercise in the administration of teacher personnel, the Massachusetts Supreme Court has defined the term as "the equitable decision of what is just and proper under the circumstances."[55]

One case is on record in which a board attempted to dismiss a permanent teacher unlawfully and then, recognizing that its action was abortive, proceeded to discharge the teacher in the required manner (supra[39]). The California Appellate Court upheld this procedure. Forced leaves of absence seem to fall in the same category as summary dismissals. A New Jersey board has been restrained from imposing a year's leave of absence[56] and a

---

[52] Nommensen v. Hoboken, N. J. S. L. D., 1928, 166 (1923).
[53] Sheldon v. Hopedale, 177 N. E. 94 (1931).
[54] More information concerning marriage cases will be presented later in this chapter (p. 110 f.).
[55] Paquette v. Fall River, 179 N. E. 588 (1931).
[56] White v. Hillsdale, N. J. S. R., 1927, 63.

Tenure Laws as Revealed by Appeal Cases   87

New York board has been enjoined from similar action in the case of a teacher subject to involuntary retirement.[57]

That the contractual rights of boards of education are not violated by indefinite tenure statutes has already been pointed out (page 75). In fact, no privileges or powers belonging to boards are lost upon the passage of protective tenure laws; their exercise, however, is more narrowly delimited and more carefully defined. In addition to the restrictions already mentioned, the laws of some states operate against justifiable transfer of teachers within systems and either prohibit or make difficult salary reductions, regardless of existing conditions. These matters, though, will be discussed in another connection.

QUESTIONS OF PROBATION

Non-retention of probationary teachers holds second place jointly with summary dismissal in the distribution of appeal cases according to type in Table XII; seventeen of each of these types are on record. Only one of the probationary cases was decided in favor of the teacher (*supra*[5]), and this was occasioned by the fact that the board had waited beyond the legal time limit for notifying the teacher that her services were not desired. Three states are represented by the seventeen cases under consideration, California, New Jersey, and New York, and the points covered by these decisions are as follows: (1) purpose of probation; (2) dismissal of probationers; (3) length of probationary period and reckoning thereof; (4) place of service; (5) rôle of contract and of board action in initiating tenure protection; and (6) effect of promotion upon teacher status.

Purpose of Probation

Only one probationary case has discussed the underlying theory of the trial service requirement, but the subject has also been given some attention by the Appellate Court of the District of Columbia.[58] The New Jersey Commissioner plainly stated in Allen *v.* Belleville[59] that the purpose of the probationary requirement is to enable a board of education to decide whether it wants

---

[57] Matter of Appeal of Pietsch, 38 N. Y. S. D. R. 17 (1928).
[58] D. C. *v.* Martin, 34 App. D. C. 265; 38 W. L. R. 18.
[59] Allen *v.* Belleville, 3 N. J. M. R. 406 (1928).

to give a teacher a permanent position. A similar viewpoint was pronounced by the District of Columbia tribunal in a non-tenure case.

The intent of Congress in prescribing that the first year in this group or class, which includes head teachers and teachers of normal, high, and manual training schools, should be probationary, was, we think, to subject the applicant for permanent appointment to a period of trial that the applicant's qualities, capacity, and desirability might be determined before final appointment. (*supra*[58])

Dismissal of Probationary Teachers

Since probationers are essentially the same as contract teachers, boards have the right to drop them at the end of a school year or to dismiss them at any time upon sufficient provocation. It is true that some indefinite tenure laws provide for the retention from one year to another of all probationers who are not notified by a stipulated date that their contracts will close at the end of the current year; however, such provisions afford no more protection than is enjoyed by teachers serving under ordinary continuous contract laws. This statement is attested by two California cases,[60] (*supra*[5]), one of which demonstrates the protective value of the continuous contract. The Appellate Court ruled in Blalock v. Ridgway (*supra*[5]) that failure of a board to notify a teacher of their intention to discontinue her services within the time limit then operative automatically granted the teacher a contract for the ensuing year.

Local boards of education in New York are vested with discretionary power to discontinue the service of teachers during probation, according to several decisions of the State Commissioner. Illustrative cases are the *Matter of Appeal of Mandigo* (*supra*[22]), in which it was held that a board has the right to dispense with any of its probationers at any time, and the *Matter of Appeal of Culver*,[61] wherein the Commissioner ruled that the appellant, a probationer, was eligible for dismissal at any time, upon recommendation of her superintendent, by a majority vote of the governing board—unless the board had waived its statutory power thus to dismiss.

Dismissal of probationary teachers in New Jersey may take place without the stating of causes, even where board rules and

[60] Fleming v. Oakville Sch. Dist., 64 Cal. App. Dec. 795 (1931).
[61] Matter of Appeal of Culver, 37 N. Y. S. D. R. 684 (1928).

regulations or contracts in force require such; however, boards that proceed in this manner are responsible for the consequences of their acts.[62]

Mr. Brisson [a probationer] was dismissed without making charges against him, and without giving him three months notice as stipulated in the contract. The Board of Education has the right to relieve Mr. Brisson of his duties as a teacher, but it is responsible for the legal consequences of its act; that is, the Board must pay Mr. Brisson full salary for the year. This was done and the obligation of the Board of Education has been fully discharged.[62]

New Jersey teacher contracts commonly contain a notification clause providing for their termination at the option of either contracting party, upon the giving of a fixed number of days' notice. The legality of this proviso has been established by decisions of appeal authorities.[63, 64]

Length of Probationary Period and Reckoning Thereof

Several appeal cases are on record in which the contesting teachers, subsequent to non-retention, claimed permanent status only to find that they had not completed their respective terms of probationary service. Such cases have arisen largely from the vagueness of the governing indefinite tenure laws with regard to certain probationary matters, and consequent misinterpretations, but may also be due in part to the tendency of some boards to evade the provisions of protective tenure statutes through technicalities. The "three consecutive years" of trial service stipulated in the New Jersey law mean calendar years, as was clearly brought out in the recent case of Carrol v. State Board (supra[20]). In this case the appellant had finished three school years of service and had held three contracts for twelve months each, two of which, however, overlapped slightly, causing the total stipulated contract time to be a few days short of three calendar years. The governing board terminated the third annual contract and was upheld in this action by all the appeal authorities in the state. In the first appeal decision on this case, it was stated

that even if such termination had been illegal, appellant could have suffered no violation of potential tenure rights since her employment terms named in the contracts if allowed to be completed on September 4, 1929, would have

[62] Brisson v. Leonia, N. J. S. L. D., 1928, 83 (1917).
[63] Mannion v. Northampton Twp., N. J. S. R., 1920, 204.
[64] White v. Riverside Twp. In Ms. (1923).

been short of the three consecutive calendar years necessary under the law to gain protection.[65]

The Commissioner further stated in his verdict that it is fortunate for the public school system that less than three calendar years will not confer tenure protection; otherwise boards would be compelled, in order to prevent the gaining of permanent status, to stop a teacher's employment prior to the completion of the third academic term. Beginning a fourth year of service, after completion of the three calendar years, does not appear to be necessary even though certain decisions, e.g., Brandes *v.* Hoboken (*supra*[19]) and Shapiro *v.* Paterson,[66] may be construed as requiring this.

That the term "year" as used in the New York indefinite tenure law also signifies twelve complete months is evidenced by the *Matter of Appeal of Livingston*,[67] wherein a teacher failed to gain permanent status in a position to which she had been promoted on probation upon finishing three consecutive school years of employment. The Wisconsin case of Nyberg *v.* Milwaukee (*supra*[2]) is the only one on record which indicates that school years have been accepted as fulfilling the legal requirement for a given number of years of employment.

Shortening of the probationary period below the general requirement for the state by local board action is possible under three existing indefinite tenure laws, to wit: those of Massachusetts, New Jersey, and New York. Leech (*supra*[12]) gives as the principle for fixing a shorter term in New Jersey definite board action with clear intent to effect the end named, basing his statement on the case of Weekley *v.* Teaneck Township.

Such action should be of affirmative character by the board in meeting assembled, and not be left to inference.[68]

It was held in the case just cited and also in another, Allen *v.* Belleville (*supra*[59]), that predating a contract cannot serve to shorten the probationary period.

Any such attempt [predating a contract] is nothing but a fiction, and in the Commissioner's opinion a fictitious period of employment is not what the Teacher's Tenure Law intended. If carried out to its logical conclusion ... the contract term could be predated three years and the protection of the

[65] Carrol *v.* Matawan, Decision of Commissioner. In Ms. (1929).
[66] Shapiro *v.* Paterson, N. J. S. R., 1925, 247.
[67] Matter of Appeal of Livingston, 37 N. Y. S. D. R. 684 (1928).
[68] Weekley *v.* Teaneck Twp. In Ms. (1929).

act thus gained at once upon a period not of actual but of fictitious employment. (*supra*[59])

Although direct, purposeful board action is required in New Jersey to reduce the length of the probationary period, a board may increase its shortened period in the case of an individual teacher simply by implication.[69]

New York boards, and presumably those of Massachusetts and New Jersey, that have fixed shorter trial periods than the maximum laid down in the indefinite tenure statute may extend their periods until they reach the maximum. When a board takes such action, the new period applies to all teachers in the service not entitled to permanent tenure at the time of the extension.[70]

To be credited toward completion of the probationary requirement, a teacher's employment must be legal employment (*supra*[66]). In New Jersey the period of service is reckoned from the dates stipulated in the teacher's contract, Carrol v. Matawan (*supra*[65]).

It is the Commissioner's opinion that, as stated in the case of Benton F. Allen vs. Belleville, "the phrase 'period of employment' as used in the tenure law means the term of employment stipulated in the teacher's contracts" and that such employment does not begin with the execution of the agreement. A contract may be signed at one time but provide for employment at a much later date and the intervening period with possible occupation elsewhere cannot consequently, in the Commissioner's opinion, possibly be considered as one of teaching employment.[65]

According to an Appeal Court decision,[71] California teachers evidently had to serve the legal trial periods after the initiation of indefinite tenure. New Jersey teachers, however, seem to have received credit for prior service (i.e., employment immediately preceding enactment of an indefinite tenure law). In Marstellar v. Pleasantville (*supra*[4]), the State Board held that a teacher had tenure protection even though serving on a contract entered into prior to the date of passage of the tenure law, and not expiring until later. Prior service was not counted toward fulfilment of the probationary requirement in New York cities that had no indefinite tenure regulations when the state law was passed.[72] Similarly, when a city in New York is incorporated and the law thus made to apply, all teachers must serve the regular proba-

[69] Ostergren v. Hoboken, N. J. S. R., 1926, 60.
[70] Matter of Appeal of Krebs, 26 N. Y. S. D. R. 353 (1921).
[71] Owens v. Santa Cruz, etc., et al., 68 Cal. App. 403 (1924).
[72] Matter of Appeal of Fayette, 21 N. Y. S. D. R. 330 (1919).

tionary period fixed by the state law or a shorter one established by the city (*supra*[22]).

Place of Service

A New Jersey decision[73] is the only one that discusses place of employment. Here it was held that the three years of probation required by law must be in the same district, but not necessarily in the same position.

The act does not, in the Commissioner's opinion, prescribe the necessary three-year period of service for each of the groups, namely, teachers, principals and supervising principals, but makes permanent the term of an incumbent whether he be teacher, principal or supervising principal, who has been employed for three consecutive years in the aggregate in the various designated positions or who has been promoted to the higher of such positions after three years of service in any one of them.[73]

Rôle of Contract and of Board Action in Initiating Tenure Protection

The fact that legal employment alone will qualify a teacher for permanent status definitely implies that probationers must either hold written contracts or be able otherwise to prove a contractual relationship. In New Jersey, official contracts are required by law only when the governing board has no rules and regulations in regard to the employment of teachers.[74] Ability to prove a contractual relationship was the deciding factor in the New Jersey case of Morrison *v.* Delaware Township,[75] wherein a board tried to demote a principal whom it had duly elected and whose services had been accepted, claiming that he did not have permanent status because he held no written contracts. The Commissioner here maintained that rendering of service which was accepted and paid for constitutes an admission of a contractual relationship and that the appellant could compel the granting of a contract, the board having failed to perform its duty. Effect of a non-valid contract is exemplified by still another New Jersey case,[76] in which a teacher failed to gain permanent status since her contract for a fourth school term was authorized by less than a majority board vote.

[73] MacNeal *v.* Ocean City, N. J. S. R., 1928, 41.
[74] Gamnon *v.* Elizabeth, N. J. S. R., 1924, 251.
[75] Morrison *v.* Delaware Twp., N. J. S. R., 1915, 59.
[76] Goble *v.* Easthampton Twp., N. J. S. R., 1927, 70.

Tenure Laws as Revealed by Appeal Cases 93

An Oregon probationary teacher not holding a duly executed contract is responsible for the consequences, according to a Supreme Court decision.[77] The plaintiff in this case having been substituted by the superintendent in charge, according to a board rule, for a teacher incapacitated by illness which resulted in death, had served in one position for three and one-half consecutive years without a written contract. Commenting on the absence of a legal contract, the Court said:

> The plaintiff had no right to rely upon the action of the superintendent as a basis of service in the capacity of teacher so as to become ultimately one of the permanently employed teachers. A knowledge of the law is imputed to her. There is no such thing as apparent scope of authority in one professing to act as agent for a public municipality of which the powers and their manner of exercise are so strictly and minutely defined by statute. . . . If one contracts with another professing to act as agent of the district, it is at the peril of the contracting party.[77]

Appeal decisions show that protected tenure ensues as a natural result of the completion of the respective probationary periods required in California, New Jersey, and Wisconsin; but that permanent appointment by the governing board is necessary in New York. In the California case of Grigsby v. King (supra[1]), the Supreme Court held that the specification of definite terms in the contracts held by the appellant did not constitute proof that she had failed to bring herself under the indefinite tenure statute then operative.

> The showing of two years successful work [the probationary period then required] brings plaintiff within the statute, and it was the duty of the board at that time to classify her as a permanent teacher, and any other action on its part was beyond its power and of no avail.[1]

An equivalent decision was rendered in the California case of LaShells v. Hench (supra[50]), where it was claimed that a teacher was not entitled to tenure protection since she had accepted yearly contracts after qualifying for protection under the statute.

Of the several New Jersey cases which show that permanent status follows immediately the completion of three consecutive calendar years of employment, the oft-cited case of Davis v. Overpeck[78] will serve well as an illustration. (This case is not the same as Davis v. Overpeck (supra[32]), although the contesting

[77] Taggart v. School Dist. No. 1, 96 Or. 422 (1920).
[78] Davis v. Overpeck Twp., N. J. S. L. D., 1928, 187, 295 (1913).

parties are identical.) Here the Supreme Court explained how the board might have prevented a principal from gaining permanent status upon serving a third term under contract.

> If the board wished to avoid the Tenure of Office Act, it could have made the term of the 1911 contract [third year] less than a year, or it could have given thirty days notice during the year, as provided in the contract, and thus cut off the employment short of three years. Not having done so, the Act of 1909 applies. (*supra*[78])

The only condition under which formal or implicit action is required of a New Jersey board is when a preceding board has given a probationer a contract for three calendar years.[79] It is universally recognized by educational and legal authorities that a ruling board of education cannot bind its successors.

Wisconsin teachers, according to a Supreme Court decision (*supra*[2]), acquire permanent status, with the substantial rights belonging thereto, simply by completing the period of probationary service, and the rights and privileges can be abrogated or disturbed only in the manner prescribed in the statute. But New York teachers, also as shown by a Supreme Court case (*supra*[8]), do not thus become automatically permanently employed. The status mentioned is obtained only by formal board appointment, upon the written recommendation of the superintendent in charge.

Effect of Promotion upon Teacher Status

Appeal cases present no direct information on this point except for New York, where teachers must serve a second probationary period upon being promoted; and the matter of promotion is mentioned only in decisions for this state and for New Jersey. Proof of the statement with regard to New York is found in the case of O'Connor v. Emerson (*supra*[47]), in which the Appellate Division of the New York Supreme Court held that

> a teacher who has served a probationary period as such, must on her appointment as principal serve another probationary period as principal and is subject to removal without hearing at any time before the termination of such period.[47]

This does not mean, however, that the incumbent loses her status as a permanent teacher when promoted.

> Her position as teacher was not lost, its tenure was simply suspended during the period of probation as principal. Upon the termination of the probation

---

[79] Davis v. Boonton, N. J. S. L. D., 1928, 141 (1925).

Tenure Laws as Revealed by Appeal Cases

it is not seen why she should be denied the rights of her position as teacher.[47]

Equivalent decisions were rendered in the *Matter of Appeal of Livingston* (*supra*[67]) and the *Matter of Appeal of Kiernan*.[80] Unlike New York teachers, the teachers of New Jersey apparently do not have to serve a second trial period following promotion (*supra*[73]).

CASES INVOLVING ADMINISTRATIVE PROBLEMS OF TRANSFER, ABOLITION OF POSITION, SUSPENSION, RESIGNATION, AND SALARY REDUCTION

Transfer Cases

Decisions of appeal authorities in transfer disputes show that unless educational employees are protected by an indefinite tenure law in particular positions, they have no protection against transfer. Generally speaking, such cases have arisen from changes of assignment which involved demotion or which were interpreted as demotions by the teachers concerned. The New York cases cited in the section just preceding are the only ones on record that may be credited to promotions; and they actually arose, not from the promotions, but from the re-transfer of the appellants to their former positions.

California boards cannot force out of the service teachers whom they consider undesirable by giving them unreasonable assignments. In Dutart v. Woodward et al.,[81] a local board transferred a woman teacher who refused to resign upon marriage to a tubercular hospital and sanitarium maintained jointly by two counties, evidently hoping to force a resignation. The Appellate Court of California here held that a permanent teacher is entitled to active employment, that classification and assignment of a teacher to specific work must be done in good faith and in accordance with the law, and that the board had no legal authority to dismiss a teacher for failing to comply with assignments of the type specified.

The inevitable result of the procedure in the present case is to accomplish by circuitous methods what the law does not directly permit.[81]

[80] Matter of Appeal of Kiernan, 36 N. Y. S. D. R. 140 (1926).
[81] Dutart v. Woodward et al., 99 Cal. App. 736 (1929).

The Oregon law now in effect provides for transfer by way of demotion only upon the consent of the teacher involved or after a hearing upon charges, if the teacher refuses to accept the new assignment.[82] But under the original law, as shown by Alexander v. School District No. 1,[83] transfer of teachers to lower positions was a power exercised by governing boards at their own discretion. In the case cited, the appellant claimed that his transfer from a principalship to a teaching position at a lower salary constituted dismissal, but the Supreme Court of Oregon held that although teachers with permanent status have the right of serving, they must serve

> in such positions and shall be subject to such assignments and transfer as the board may from time to time determine, or as may be provided for in its rules.[83]

A similar decision was rendered in the recent Massachusetts case of Boody v. Barnstable,[84] the Supreme Court holding that dismissal as contemplated by the indefinite tenure statute is complete separation, not change of assignment or lessened authority, etc.; and that the law does not create "principals" distinct from teachers, "'principals' being teachers intrusted by the school committee with special duties of direction or management."

It is noted in the case of Davis v. Overpeck (*supra*[78]) that the New Jersey indefinite tenure act makes no reference to transfer of a teacher or principal to another position, yet this case and a number of others bear witness that transfers may be made provided the teachers affected are not lowered in rank. In Cheesman v. Gloucester City[85] the Commissioner ruled that the transfer of the appellant from principalship of the seventh and eighth grades to principalship of the fifth and sixth grades was not a demotion; and the legality of this decision was upheld by both the State Board and the Supreme Court. The following comment anent transfers appears in the Commissioner's decision:

> This department has frequently decided that teachers under tenure may be transferred from one grade to another in the elementary grades without violation of the intent of the Tenure of Service Law. That is to say, a teacher in any of the elementary grades, as for instance the eighth grade,

[82] School Laws of Oregon, 1931, Chap. XXVI, Sec. 35-2606.
[83] Alexander v. Sch. Dist. No. 1, 84 Or. 172 (1917).
[84] Boody v. Barnstable, 177 N. E. 78 (1931).
[85] Cheesman v. Gloucester City, N. J. S. L. D., 1928, 156 (1923).

Tenure Laws as Revealed by Appeal Cases

may be transferred to any of the positions in the elementary grades without any violation of law. (*supra*[85])

As might be inferred, a teacher who has taught a single subject in the elementary grades, e.g., drawing, may be legally transferred to a position where she will teach all subjects in a single elementary grade.[86]

The attitude of New Jersey appeal authorities toward transfers which are, in effect, demotions, even though they produce no change in salaries, is nicely demonstrated by the case of Morrison *v.* Delaware Township (*supra*[75]), in which the Commissioner ruled, with order for reinstatement, that the transfer of a principal teacher to a subordinate position in a single room school, salary remaining constant, was tantamount to dismissal. Basis for this decision was found in the similar prior case of Davis *v.* Overpeck (*supra*[78]), wherein the State Board averred that the local board had attempted by transfer of the appellant to evade the indefinite tenure statute. The Board further pointed out that to construe the law in such fashion as to permit action of the type named would be to leave local boards free to pay the salary of principals to favorite teachers (effecting this by elevation and subsequent demotion) and to

so degrade and humiliate worthy principals that the protection which the statute is supposed to afford them would really become a myth.[78]

According to the New Jersey case of Welch *v.* West Orange,[87] it is necessary for a teacher to prove that she has held a certain position in order to be protected against transfer to a lower one. The appellant in this case was unable to show proof and therefore had to submit to demotion. Teachers may not be demoted, however, on the claim that their original appointments were in violation of board rules and consequently were illegal.[88]

Although the New Jersey law provides for dismissal of teachers on abolition of positions, local boards sometimes effect transfers instead. In Kuyl *v.* Paterson[89] an art supervisor protested against transfer to a regular teaching position, upon abolition of the supervisory post, with the result that the transfer was termed entirely legal. And in Tobey *v.* Newark,[90] a similar case, the

[86] Shroder *v.* Irvington, N. J. S. R., 1919, 216.
[87] Welch *v.* West Orange, N. J. S. L. D., 1928, 197 (1914).
[88] Noonan and Arnot *v.* Paterson, N. J. S. R., 1925, 277.
[89] Kuyl *v.* Paterson, N. J. S. R., 1925, 288.
[90] Tobey *v.* Newark, N. J. S. L. D., 1928, 161 (1914).

Commissioner stated that the appellant could have been dismissed and that the transfer was, therefore, not a transfer but an appointment to a position then vacant.

Abolition of Position

Appeal authorities agree that local boards may abolish positions when occasion demands, acting in good faith, without making any provision for the incumbents. A general statement appearing in a New York decision[91] epitomizes the attitude of authorities in the several states.

> The statutory provision conferring power on the board of education to abolish a position is not in conflict with the teachers' tenure law. Under similar statutes it has been held that tenure relates only to the right to continue in the position while such position exists, and that when it is abolished and no similar position has been established the former occupant has no enforceable claim for continuance in employment. This asumes that the board has acted in good faith in abolishing the position and has not indulged in a subterfuge to avoid the provisions of the tenure law for the purpose of dispensing with the services of a teacher whose services are no longer desired.[91]

The matter of bad faith was considered by the Supreme Judicial Court of Massachusetts in two cases, decided together, which arose from the combination of a junior and a senior high school principalship, and the abolition, supposedly on account of this change in organization, of an assistant senior high school principalship and a junior high school principalship, both incumbents being retained as teachers. In the former case[92] the Court held that at least two members of the school committee had been actuated by political prejudice and ill will, engendered by the political views of the petitioner, but that in the latter[93] no personal hostility was shown. Accordingly, the one appellant was ordered reinstated and the petition of the other dismissed.

Causes warranting abolition of position mentioned in indefinite tenure statutes are natural diminution of pupils and purposes of economy. The first of these is well defined in the New Jersey case of Tobey v. Newark (supra[90]).

> The correct and reasonable construction of the term "natural diminution in the number of pupils" is that whenever the number of pupils enrolled in the

[91] Matter of Appeal of Mack, 30 N. Y. S. D. R. 154 (1923).
[92] Pollard v. Sch. Committee of Revere, 249 Mass. 525 (1924).
[93] Sweeney v. Revere, 249 Mass. 525 (1924).

Tenure Laws as Revealed by Appeal Cases

schools is decreased either by an actual loss of population, or by reason of discontinuing a class and sending the pupils to another school, thereby rendering the services of the teacher of such class unnecessary, there has been a "natural diminution" within the meaning of the law. (*supra*[90])

No definition of economy is found in appeal decisions, but several do offer it as a cause of abolition. In the New Jersey controversy of Fitzherbert v. Roxbury Township,[94] which resulted from the closing of a one-room school, the Commissioner denied the petition of the appellant for a position in Roxbury Township and defended consolidation of small schools on the ground that it makes for greater efficiency and economy in the school system.

Two New Jersey cases have presented the question of whether or not a position had been abolished. In Mills v. Washington[95] a high school principal who did some work in connection with the elementary grades appealed from being deprived of a position as the result of legal closing of a two-year high school. The Commissioner refused this appeal and defined abolition of position in so doing.

.... it is the Commissioner's opinion that a position may be considered as abolished when so many elements are removed therefrom that there no longer substantially exists the office or position to which the incumbent was appointed and for which his services were originally desired.[95]

The other case referred to above turned upon the legality of the vote taken by the Board, the Commissioner holding that abolition action is legal only when approved by a majority of the local board and not by a majority of a quorum.[96]

Suspension

Temporary suspension of teachers either as a disciplinary measure or as an expedient while trial proceedings are being started has figured in but a few appeal cases. The right of local boards in California to use suspension as a disciplinary measure was established by the case of Goldsmith v. Sacramento City,[97] which had to do with the suspension of a teacher for unprofessional conduct. It was urged by the appellant that temporary suspension was illegal since the indefinite tenure statute then operative did not expressly provide for it; but the Appellate Court took a dif-

[94] Fitzherbert v. Roxbury Twp., N. J. S. R., 1916, 193.
[95] Mills v. Washington Twp. In Ms. (1929).
[96] Tomlin v. Glassboro, 1 N. J. M. R. 568 (1923).
[97] Goldsmith v. Sacramento City et al., 66 Cal. App. 157 (1924).

ferent view of the matter, holding that the word "dismiss" includes the word "suspend," according to the established legal maxim "the greater contains the less."

So interpreting, then, the word "dismiss," and as it is believed the legislature intended it should be understood and so used, the section [indefinite tenure] vests in the board the discretion of determining, in any given or particular case, whether the accused teacher should be permanently or temporarily dismissed. (*supra*[97])

The only other state where temporary suspension has been used for disciplinary purposes, according to appeal decisions, is New York, and here the measure was adopted not by a local board, but by the Commissioner in commuting a dismissal decision imposed on two teachers who had assisted with the issuance and circulation of a pamphlet attacking and ridiculing the administration of the Buffalo city schools (*supra*[38]). Here the Commissioner held that disciplinary action was justified, but that certain mitigating circumstances, i.e., long experience and satisfactory service save for the indiscretion cited, also substantial rights and privileges in the city and state teachers' retirement funds, which would be materially affected, or even destroyed, by permanent dismissal, justified alleviation of the punishment. Accordingly, the Commissioner, after iterating his discretionary power to direct the modification of an order or decision of a local board, directed the reinstatement of the appellants after a given period.

Suspension is possible in New Jersey only pending hearing of dismissal charges. In Conway v. Edgewater[98] the Commissioner ruled that suspension, not being mentioned in the indefinite tenure act, is inconsistent with said act and therefore illegal.

The law does not contemplate the punishment of supervising principals, who have attained tenure, by suspending them. If the conduct of a supervising principal or teacher under tenure is unbecoming to the profession, such principal or teacher may be dismissed and . . . suspension may be included in a dismissal pending the hearing.[98]

This position was reaffirmed in Rein v. Riverside Township.[99]

Resignation

The matter of resignations, like that of suspensions, has been given only slight consideration in appeal cases. It has been

[98] Conway v. Edgewater, N. J. S. R., 1928, 101.
[99] Rein v. Riverside Twp. In Ms. (1931).

Tenure Laws as Revealed by Appeal Cases

decided by the Commissioner of New Jersey, however, that if a teacher resigns and is immediately reëlected, the effect of the resignation is to cut the teacher off from tenure protection.[100]

<small>The Appellant in this case was supervising principal of the schools in Madison Township, Middlesex County, up to February 3, 1916. At that time he resigned and was immediately reappointed to the same position. No one pretends to know or say why he resigned, not even the Appellant himself, but the effect of his resignation was to cut him off from the benefit of the tenure of service act.[100]</small>

Unlike New Jersey teachers, educational employees of California are protected against the tendency of some local boards to resort to collusive resignations in order to prevent the accrual of permanent status. In a recent opinion,[101] the Attorney General of the state ruled that boards cannot make agreements with third-year probationers to reëmploy them after they have resigned and thus produced breaks in their service records.

Two cases have occurred in New Jersey in which a resignation was filed under one board to take effect after the assuming of office by a new board. The Supreme Court held in Nicholson v. Swedesboro,[102] reversing decisions of the Commissioner and State Board, that the governing board at the time the resignation was submitted could accept the request even though it was without power to fill the vacancy. An equivalent decision was rendered by state educational authorities in the later case of Shaver v. Avalon.[103]

Apparent refusal to sign a contract, said contract calling for a lower compensation than the teacher had been receiving, has been termed tantamount to a resignation by the California Appellate Court.[104]

Salary Reduction

Tenure controversies resulting from decreases in salary have occurred in California, Massachusetts, and New Jersey. Teachers in the first-named state have no protection against lowering of salaries, according to Fidler v. Roseville (*supra*[104]), in which the appellant claimed that the local board had no right to change his

<small>[100] Fountain v. Madison Twp., N. J. S. R., 1917, 298.
[101] *Sierra Ed. News*, Vol. 27, No. 14, p. 45, Sept. 1931.
[102] Nicholson v. Swedesboro, N. J. S. R., 1912, 96; 83 N. J. L. 36 (1912).
[103] Shaver v. Avalon, N. J. S. R., 1927, 46.
[104] Fidler v. Roseville Union H. S., 64 Cal. App. Dec. 851 (1931).</small>

salary. The Appellate Court held that the trustees in question had the power to regulate the compensation of teachers in the schools, whether the effect was to raise or lower salaries, and that they could decrease the petitioner's salary for the succeeding year provided the new figure constituted reasonable pay for the services to be performed.

Under a salary provision[105] of the Massachusetts school code, reduction of salary is possible only when a general revision applying to all teachers of the same class, or grade, is made. A protest against such a revision was made in Paquette *v.* Fall River (*supra*[55]) since the reduction did not affect several contract teachers. Here the Supreme Judicial Court ruled that the statute under which teachers are employed to serve at the discretion of school committees governs compensation as well as tenure; that the contract teachers in question were not of the same class as the others; and that the action of the board was entirely legal.

In deciding whether a general salary revision affects all such teachers, not only must consideration be given to "salary" received, but also to the sum of the factors comprehended within the scope of "grade" . . . .[55]

Several transfer cases already cited (pages 96 f.) and a few decisions that will be treated here show clearly the effect of the mandatory salary regulations in the New Jersey indefinite tenure law. Neither the salary of an individual teacher nor those of a group can be legally reduced. Changing of annual salary payments from ten monthly installments to twelve has also been held illegal.[106]

The prosecutrix had served three consecutive years as school teacher in the public schools of Paterson and, therefore, holds her employment during good behavior and efficiency and is not subject to a reduction of salary. A resolution by the board of education changing the mode of payments from 10 equal monthly payments to 12, and which in effect clearly reduces her salary, is in clear violation of the section.[106]

Temporary salary increases do not permanently obligate a local board in New Jersey.[107] The reason for this was given by the State Board in its decision on the case cited, as well as the purpose of the mandatory salary provision of the indefinite tenure law:

---

[105] General Laws Relating to Ed., Mass., 1927, Chap. 71, Sec. 43.
[106] Gowdy *v.* St. Bd. of Ed. et al., 84 N. J. L. 231; 85 N. J. L. 726 (1913).
[107] Reed & Hills *v.* Trenton, N. J. S. R., 1917, 309.

Tenure Laws as Revealed by Appeal Cases 103

If the statute were so construed any and all temporary payments to teachers for temporary work could not be made without incurring the liability of a permanent indebtedness and school boards would be tempted to put all extra service upon teachers without any extra compensation whatever.

The prohibition of the statute was meant to prevent school boards from reducing a teacher's salary to a nominal sum and thus forcing a resignation that could not be gotten otherwise. (*supra*[107])

Refusal of a board to grant salary increments to married women teachers was the issue in Morgenweck et al. *v.* Gloucester,[108] in which the State Board decided against the several appellants, reasoning thus:

It seems improbable that the knowledge that a salary might not be increased would restrain a woman from marriage when the salary she was receiving before marriage would be continued to her and become a supplement to the salary of her husband. The Commissioner must, therefore, conclude that this discrimination so far as single and married women teachers are concerned is not against public policy.[108]

Another New Jersey salary increment case is that of Samuelsen *v.* Edgewater,[109] wherein the Commissioner ruled that the appellant was not eligible for an expected annual increase since she had not met board requirements for such.

CASES ARISING LARGELY FROM DISMISSAL FOLLOWING CHARGES

Previous sections of this chapter have dealt chiefly with the major characteristics of indefinite tenure laws and their effects and with appeal cases arising from claimed or real violation of tenure rights, in which the local boards acted without presentation of charges. This division will treat mainly cases eventuating from removal of teachers after charges and hearings, according to law. These cases group themselves under the following heads: (1) inefficiency and incompetency; (2) incapacity; (3) unbecoming and unprofessional conduct; (4) insubordination; (5) other just cause; and (6) miscellaneous, which embraces marriage cases, suits for salary, questions of leave, and other infrequently occurring types.

Inefficiency and Incompetency

Although charges of inefficiency and incompetency have occurred frequently in appeal cases, they have almost always been presented

---
[108] Morgenweck et al. *v.* Gloucester City. In Ms. (1930).
[109] Samuelsen *v.* Edgewater, *Ed. Bul.* (N. J.), Vol. 18, No. 4, p. 237, Dec. 1931.

in conjunction with other charges, and decisions in such cases have fallen considerably short of adequate definition of the two terms. The Commissioner of Education of New Jersey attempted to define teaching efficiency in Davis v. Overpeck (*supra*[32]).

> In considering the case of the Appellant as to his efficiency as a teacher, it is proper to consider what are the main qualities of an efficient teacher. It will perhaps be agreed that there are four that he must possess. First, he must have adequate knowledge of the subjects which he is teaching; second, he should have reasonable skill; third, he should have sufficient personality to inspire pupils to the further pursuit of knowledge and education after leaving the high school; fourth, he should be industrious in the work which he attempts to do.[32]

And again in Marstellar v. Pleasantville,[110] where a supervising principal was concerned, the same officer said:

> In order to warrant the discharge of a teacher or principal on the general charge of inefficiency it must be clearly proven that unsatisfactory condition of the class or school is due to the inability of the teacher or principal, against whom charges are preferred, to impart instruction, maintain discipline, and work in harmony with the teachers with whom he is associated.[110]

Specific and general characteristics of the services of employees have been stated in a few New Jersey cases where inefficiency was one of the major charges. Thus in Hamilton v. Irvington,[111] the facts cited as evidence of inefficiency and unbecoming conduct on the part of a supervising principal were: (1) lateness in opening school without acceptable reason therefor; (2) an inadequate supervisory program and failure to meet the school superintendent's requirement in regard to this; and (3) failure to perform routine work. Too little time spent in supervision was also the reason for removal of another supervising principal, the State Board holding that

> the visiting of a school a day from fifteen minutes to an hour and a half does not constitute adequate or sufficient supervision on the part of a supervising principal whose whole time is supposed to be devoted to his office. . . . The duty of a supervising principal is primarily the supervision of instruction in the classroom. (*supra*[100])

Absence of a supervisory program or of any other system to help teachers and the fact that the schools were not up to standard, in fact were actually deteriorating, were the reasons given for dis-

[110] Marstellar v. Pleasantville, N. J. S. R., Vol. 1, 1913, 246.
[111] Hamilton v. Irvington, N. J. S. R., 1929, 860.

Tenure Laws as Revealed by Appeal Cases 105

missal of yet another supervising principal, the sole charge being inefficiency (*supra*[35]). And, finally, persistent tardiness in opening school, after warnings by board members, has been termed sufficient cause for dismissing a teacher on charges of inefficiency, incompetency, and insubordination.[112]

The Commissioner of Education of New York has agreed that issuance and circulation of a pamphlet by an organization of teachers attacking and ridiculing the school administration constitutes, among other things, failure to give efficient and competent service (*supra*[38]). He held in this instance that the conduct of those teachers responsible for the action named was reprehensible and that disciplinary action was in order, but ruled that temporary suspension was drastic enough. In another New York case,[113] the same authority adjudged absence from duty as inefficient and incompetent service.

> It is not "good behavior," within the meaning of the statute, for a teacher to absent herself, without reasonable excuse, from her position, since, although there be no rule or regulation prohibiting such absence, it constitutes necessarily a breach of the obligations attached to her position. It is obvious that there could be no efficiency of school administration if teachers,of their own accord, were permitted to leave their places for the purpose of engaging in political, social or individual activities, in no way connected with the teaching services which they are employed to perform.[113]

Strong pacifistic views have also been held to make a New York teacher inefficient and incompetent (*supra*[44]).

Incapacity

No attempt to define incapacity appears in any appeal cases and this charge has played a major rôle in only one case (*supra*[33]). In this dispute a New Jersey teacher urged that as the wearing of glasses is permitted to improve vision, so should the wearing of an acousticon be allowed for improvement of defective hearing. But the State Board, pointing out that the acousticon is not the equal of the normal ear, held that the dismissal of said teacher was legal.

The Commissioner of Education of New Jersey has held in a contract tenure case where incapacity was claimed that the board in question had no right to deny a teacher the opportunity to

---
[112] Blackus *v.* Delaware Twp., N. J. S. R., 1912, 122.
[113] Matter of Appeal of Fotheringham, 15 N. Y. S. D. R. 498 (1918).

perform her duties "in the absence of an actual demonstration of her physical unfitness."[114]

Unbecoming Conduct

Grounds which have caused the dismissal of teachers for unbecoming conduct are: (1) infliction of corporal punishment; (2) breach of professional ethics; (3) transgression of generally accepted social and moral codes; and (4) unpatriotic attitudes and activities. Appeal cases of the first three types have occurred only in New Jersey and of the last type, in New York alone.

As is shown by Schermerhorn v. Hanover Township,[115] no serious infliction of corporal punishment is required to justify a New Jersey board in dismissing a teacher for this cause.

> It is not sufficient to plead that few of the children testified that they were hurt, and only one stated the punishment was such as to make him cry.[115]

Another case in which something akin to corporal punishment was the main issue is that of Smith v. Phillipsburg (*supra*[31]), in which a teacher was dismissed for using his foot to "push" a pupil, as he said, and to "kick" him, as friends of the boy and the boy himself claimed, toward the principal's office. The Commissioner here upheld the decision of the local board, after commenting that the fundamental question at stake was whether or not the action was unbecoming.

> The boy was not injured, but the insult, the humiliation, quite as much as the injury, must be considered.[31]

Overstepping the bounds of professional ethics as ground for dismissal is illustrated by Hamilton v. Irvington (*supra*[111]), wherein it is stated that borrowing money from teachers or janitors, or selling them stock, or being slow in paying one's own bills or school bills is unbecoming conduct. With regard to delinquent debt payments, the decision said:

> This fact [slowness in paying school bills], together with the fact that through his own numerous obligations or those of his wife which he had assumed, he was known throughout the community to be constantly in financial arrears, was bound to impair his high standing as a school principal and his usefulness as such and to reflect indirectly discredit on the Irvington school system.[111]

---

[114] Vetter v. Galloway Twp. In Ms. (1929).
[115] Schermerhorn v. Hanover Twp., N. J. S. R., 1920, 192.

Clandestine meetings with a woman other than his wife, avowedly for the purpose of helping this individual heal the ills of her own family, resulted in the dismissal of a principal in Hoboken, New Jersey.[116] The Commissioner's conclusion in this case was:

> The important question in the final analysis is, are the explanations of the clandestine meetings and the unusual situations in which the Appellant was found consistent with good morals, professional fidelity, and the common standard of social ethics. The Board of Education decided without a dissenting vote that these explanations were inconsistent and found Mr. Oliver guilty of conduct unbecoming a teacher. As a result he was dismissed from service as principal of the school. It is my opinion that this conclusion was a fair one.[116]

Several tenure controversies involving questions of patriotism arose in New York during the World War and one has occurred since that time. The general charge brought in these various cases has not always been the same, i.e., unbecoming conduct, but the decisions have all been of a kind; which is to say that they have held that public education is an expression of government and that teachers are the servants of the state and must give undivided allegiance at all times to the state. This idea is well set forth in the following excerpt from the *Matter of Appeal of Mufson, Schneer, and Schmalhausen* (*supra*[6]), which was the first appeal case of the type under consideration:

> The schools of America should be an expression of American ideals, of her democratic institutions and of her philosophy of life and of representative government. There has not been a time in the history of the country when the public schools should be engaged more persistently, scientifically and patriotically in teaching the fundamental principles of America's philosophy of life and government than at the present time. A person who does not, without reservation, utilize all his intellectual powers and exert all his influence as a teacher in the public schools to make such schools an efficient and effective agency in the accomplishment of this great function of a school system is not a suitable person to be charged with the duties of the sacred office of teacher.[6]

The appellants in this case held that they had been unlawfully dismissed since the indefinite tenure law makes no provision for dismissal of teachers for unbecoming conduct, but the Acting Commissioner ruled otherwise, defining the charge in so doing.

> Conduct on the part of a teacher which is sufficient cause for removal is "conduct unbecoming a teacher." While the law does not specifically provide

[116] *Oliver v. Hoboken*, N. J. S. R., 1917, 305.

for the removal of a teacher for "conduct unbecoming a teacher," it is entirely proper, and within the causes for which charges may be preferred, for the school authorities to prefer charges against a teacher for "conduct unbecoming a teacher." (*supra*⁶)

Statement is also made in the case from which the preceding quotations were taken that teachers have a right to their own individualities and opinions; however, the effect of this argument is partially offset by a qualifying statement to the end that there was no difference of opinion among patriotic citizens regarding prosecution of the World War and likewise that there were no varying views concerning the obligation of teachers to support the government and to teach love and respect for democratic institutions and for the president of the Republic.

The single case of deficient patriotism occurring after the close of the World War had to do with a teacher who was charged with applying for membership in the Communist Party and actively engaging in its work.[117] In this dispute the Commissioner upheld the local board in removal of the teacher, averring that direct or indirect participation by a servant of the state in the activities of any organization seeking by violence or other unlawful means to overturn the government forfeits her right to tenure protection.

Unprofessional Conduct

Political activity within the school, i.e., advocacy before a class of a certain candidate for county superintendent of schools, is the only specific act that has been interpreted as unprofessional conduct by an appeal authority (*supra*⁹⁷). The Appellate Court of California defended the temporary suspension sentence imposed by the local board in this case and, in so doing, delivered itself of some important opinions concerning the charge of unprofessional conduct. It was claimed by the appellant here that the term "unprofessional conduct" is so general, so undefined, so vague as to make meaning indeterminable—that any act might constitute it, and that to make this ground valid was to make teachers' employment dependent upon the whim and caprice of local boards. In answer to this, the Court upheld the generality of the charge, calling attention to the fact that it would be impossible for the law to state all that might come under this and defending the power of discretion thus left to local boards.

[117] Matter of Appeal of Pratt, 25 N. Y. S. D. R. 65 (1921).

If "unprofessional conduct" as a ground of dismissal is void because it leaves too much to the judgment or discretion of the Board of Education in determining what constitutes it, then "immoral conduct," "incompetence," and "evident unfitness for teaching" must likewise be held void for the same reason and practically all of the vitally necessary power of the boards will be stripped from them. A decision which involved such radical consequences should be reluctantly arrived at and reached only for reasons which are unanswerable. (*supra*[97])

The Court further stated in this case that teachers must conform to the customs of communities in which they teach and order their private and public lives in agreement with such prevailing modes of conduct.

In a New Jersey case where unprofessional conduct, insubordination, and conduct unbecoming of a teacher were charged—specific accusations being that the teacher disregarded the known rules of the local board, failed to serve the children as shown by frequent late openings and early closings of school, and kept improperly her school register—the Commissioner held that the local board was justified in its finding for dismissal.[118]

Other Just Cause

Although a number of appeal cases might well be placed in this category, i.e., many of those that follow in the miscellaneous section, very little information regarding the meaning or scope of the charge can be got from appeal decisions, except by inference. The only definition of "cause" appears in a New York decision (*supra*[6]).

The meaning of the word "cause" is well settled. It means some substantial, reasonable, valid cause; some action or conduct on the part of a teacher which renders his services undesirable or prevents him from exercising the wholesome influence which a teacher should exercise over his pupils. Such conduct is "conduct unbecoming a teacher."[6]

Leech (*supra*[12]) classifies insubordination and neglect of duty cases under "other just cause," and perhaps with good reason, for the New Jersey indefinite tenure law makes no provision for these charges; still the writer is of the opinion that the charge of insubordination is important enough to merit a separate head and that the charge of neglect of duty naturally falls under other heads.

[118] Van Horn *v.* Hope Twp. In Ms. (1922).

Insubordination

Information regarding insubordination cases comes from New Jersey alone. In Gebhart v. Hopewell (*supra*[51]), a teacher was adjudged guilty of insubordination because of repeated failure to report at the school at times directed by the high school principal and the supervising principal and "for failure, refusal and neglect to file reports and furnish information as and when requested by the high school principal." Two other cases of insubordination, resulted from transfers involving demotions. The first of these cases, in point of time, had to do with a teacher of commercial subjects who accepted with poor grace assignment to clerical duties in the supervising principal's office and who was dismissed several months after the transfer for inefficiency, incompetency, neglect of duty, and insubordination.[119] Here the Commissioner held that it was not insubordination for the teacher to refuse to perform the new duties since a demotion was involved. A very different conclusion was reached by the State Board and the Supreme Court in the other, and later, decision (*supra*[85]), which arose from the refusal of a teacher to accept a new assignment. The Court held here that the teacher was guilty of insubordination in refusing to obey the order of the local board, that the appellant should have accepted the transfer under protest pending an appeal, and that such action would not have prejudiced her appeal.

Miscellaneous

Since a goodly number of the cases listed under this head in Table XII have already been cited in connection with other sections of this chapter, there remain for treatment here only the questions of marriage of women teachers, suits for salary lost during illegal suspensions or removals from office, and attempts to waive or to confer tenure. As has already been stated (pages 85 f.), appeal authorities in all states where the issue has arisen, except Massachusetts, have held that women teachers cannot be removed or forced to resign from their positions upon marriage or upon passage of board rules prohibiting employment of married women teachers. Arguments given in decisions ordering the reinstatement of dismissed married women teachers are that indefinite tenure laws do not specify marriage as a cause for removal, that

[119] Gamnon v. Leonia, N. J. S. R., 1921, 310.

marriage in itself does not constitute any of the approved charges, and that it is a well-established social custom, fostered by a sound public policy. The following expression from a decision rendered by the New York Commissioner of Education typifies the attitudes of appeal authorities in general:

> It seems clear to me . . . that to declare either by legislative act or an administrative rule that the marriage of a teacher unfits her for public service would be opposed to existing public policy and would be an unfair discrimination against married women. If a married woman possesses the required qualifications and performs her duties with the same degree of competency and efficiency as an unmarried woman it would be not only unjust but I think illegal to discriminate against her because of marriage.[120]

Appeal decisions asserting the right of married women teachers to their positions have been handed down in California, the District of Columbia, Maryland, New Jersey, New York, and Oregon.

In the only Massachusetts case in point (*supra*[53]), the Supreme Judicial Court held that, all provisions of the law having been complied with, the elimination of a teacher subsequent to the passage of a board rule forbidding employment of married women on the teaching force was entirely legal. The Court commented upon the ruling of the local board thus:

> A decision that wise administration of public schools calls for the elimination of women teachers if they are married is not so irrational that it is inconsistent in law with good faith in dealing with a question of dismissal.[53]

The trend of decisions in suits for salary lost during illegal suspensions, whether intended as temporary or permanent, shows an advantage for the teacher. In the New Jersey case of Tomlin v. Glassboro (*supra*[96]), a local board was ordered to pay the salary of a dismissed teacher from the time of dismissal to the date of legal discontinuance of the course he taught. The New York Commissioner has also ordered the payment of salary lost during an illegal suspension[121] as has the Appellate Court of California (*supra*[49]). But in another case[122] this same Court ruled against a reinstated teacher's plea for lost salary on the ground that the district was enjoined from incurring debts in excess of current income without approval of two-thirds of the qualified electors. There is also a question as to whether the writ of man-

---
[120] Matter of Appeal of Thomas, 33 N. Y. S. D. R. 12 (1925).
[121] Matter of Appeal of Wade, 40 N. Y. S. D. R. 44 (1930).
[122] Martin v. Fisher et al., 108 Cal. App. 34 (1930).

damus granted by the Supreme Court of California in Saxton *v.* Los Angeles (*supra*[43]) carried with it an order for lost salary as well as for reinstatement.

Inability of local boards to confer tenure rights on teachers by predating contracts has already been discussed (pages 90 f.). Similarly, it is impossible for a superintendent to confer permanent status upon a teacher.[123] Waiving of tenure rights once they have come into existence is also just as emphatically denied by appeal authorities. In 1924 the Attorney General of New Jersey rendered an opinion on the indefinite tenure law, at the request of the Assistant Commissioner of Education, in which he held that the purpose of the Tenure Act cannot be defeated by the procedure mentioned.[124] This opinion was used by the Commissioner in White *v.* Hillsdale (*supra*[56]), in which waiver of tenure was claimed, and in an equivalent decision, Tomlin *v.* Glassboro (*supra*[96]). The Commissioner of Education of New York has given his opinion that waiving of tenure protection is contrary to public policy, stating that if such action were allowed the indefinite tenure law would have but slight significance (*supra*[7]).

SELECTED REFERENCES

Bibliographic Guide

AMERICAN DIGEST. West Publishing Company, Saint Paul, Minnesota.
  Second Decennial Edition, 1907-1916, Vol. XX.
  Third Decennial Edition, 1917-1926, Vol. XXI.
  Current Digests, 1927-1931.

Legal Sources

FEDERAL REPORTS.
NATIONAL REPORTER SYSTEM. West Publishing Company, Saint Paul, Minnesota.
  Atlantic Reporter.
  Northeastern Reporter.
  Northwestern Reporter.
  Pacific Reporter.
NEW JERSEY
  Annual Reports of the State Board of Education and of the Commissioner of Education.
  School Law Decisions.
  Supplement to School Law Decisions.

[123] Ackerman *v.* Phillipsburg, N. J. S. R., 1926, 78.
[124] *Ed. Bul., N. J.,* Vol. 11, No. 2, pp. 46-47, Oct. 1924.

NEW YORK
  Annual Reports of the State Department of Education. State Reporter Systems.

Magazine Articles

BEARER, E. V. "A Digest of Trials Held in New Jersey Under Permanent Tenure Law." *University of Pennsylvania Ninth Annual Schoolmen's Week Proceedings*, 1922, pp. 220-26.

HOUSMAN, IDA E. "Evaluating the New Jersey Tenure Law by the Decisions." *American School Board Journal*, 67:53-54, September 1923.

———. "Decisions Under the New Jersey Tenure Law." *Education Bulletin* (N. J.), 16:17-23, September 1929.

LENTZ, A. E. "More About Tenure." *Sierra Educational News*, 27:44-45, September 1931.

SHAFER, PAUL R. and O'MARA, THOMAS. "The Teacher Tenure Law in the Courts." *Indiana Teacher*, 75:26, November 1930.

Research Study

LEECH, CARL G. *The Constitutional and Legal Basis of Education in New Jersey.* Ph.D. Dissertation, University of Pennsylvania, 1932.

CHAPTER VI

Comparison of Teacher Tenure and Certain Related Aspects of Teacher Personnel Regulations and Practices in Six European Countries with Similar Provisions and Conditions Existing in the American States Having Indefinite Tenure Laws

THAT indefinite teacher tenure is practically universal in Europe and has been in existence there as long as public education, has come to be common knowledge among educators of the United States; but only limited information, and this in scattered sources, has been available concerning its provision and operation in the various countries. Very nearly all references to the topic in American educational literature take the form of broad generalizations, of which the following frequently-quoted statement of President Charles W. Eliot is a good example:

> The American schools will never equal the schools of Germany and France until well-proved teachers can secure a tenure during behavior and efficiency like teachers in those countries.[1]

A more recent comment refers to the universality of indefinite tenure in Europe and concludes that

> The American practice of appointing teachers one year at a time would not be tolerated, because it would tend to destroy the security, contentment and esprit de corps so necessary in successful teaching.[2]

The only serious attempt to study teacher tenure conditions in European countries was made in 1924 by the Tenure Committee of One Hundred of the National Education Association and the results reported in a regular issue of the *Research Bulletin*[3] published by the Association. Information for this study was secured entirely by the questionnaire method from the embassies in Wash-

---
[1] Quoted by Arrowwood, C. F., in "Permanent Membership in the Teaching Profession," *Sch. and Soc.*, Vol. 28, p. 177, Aug. 11, 1928.
[2] Quotation from the *Indiana Teacher* appearing in *Common Ground*, Vol. 6, No. 8, p. 261, May 1927.
[3] "The Problem of Teacher Tenure," *N. E. A. Research Bul.*, Vol. 2, No. 5, Nov. 1924.

ington of those European countries having a higher literacy rank than the United States,[4] the points covered being provisions for appointment, tenure, and dismissal of teachers. Conclusions reached were as follows:

... teachers in the educational systems of European countries, where a high degree of school development has taken place, are much more completely protected by tenure than are teachers in the United States. No such policy as the "hire and fire" practice, common in many of our States, exists, neither is there such a thing as a "yearly contract" plan of election for teachers.
... the teaching profession in those countries, in which illiteracy is very nearly abolished, seems to be upon a very stable basis. The itemized tenure provisions, enumerated by the embassies for their respective countries, show that age retirement with pension seems almost universal. Furthermore no distinction is made between executives, supervisors, and teachers in tenure and dismissal provisions.[5]

Being unable to locate detailed information regarding teacher tenure and related aspects of teacher personnel regulations and practices in the leading countries of Europe, the writer undertook an investigation which embraced six countries: England and Wales, France, Germany, Italy, Norway, and Sweden.[6] These countries were chosen partly because they appeared to be representative of Europe in general, at least as far as teacher personnel practices are concerned, and partly because desired facts were more readily available for them than for other countries. They all have highly centralized systems of education with the single exception of England and Wales, where equally as much local autonomy exists as in the states of the United States.

The major aim of this study was to assemble, from legal sources and research studies, data that would make possible a comparison of the essential features of tenure requirements and practices in the six European countries with corresponding facts for the American states having indefinite tenure laws. Topics on which information was collected were as follows: (1) training required of all public school teachers; (2) procedure of appointment, i.e., appointing authority, probationary period, and transfers; (3) tenure of office and disciplinary regulations; and (4) salary and pension

[4] The countries included were: Denmark, Finland, France, Germany, Great Britain, Netherlands, Norway, Sweden, and Switzerland.
[5] Footnote Ref. No. 3, pp. 156-57.
[6] All of these countries except Italy were included in the National Education Association study.

provisions. In this connection, it was also necessary to gather certain new factual material for the American states, since other phases of the entire study had concentrated attention almost entirely on the second and third of the four topics listed.

A comparative treatment of the results of the writer's research is presented in the remainder of this chapter. Facts as set forth purport to show only the main features of prevailing tenure and related personnel regulations and practices. For instance, in the case of teacher training the general qualifications for regular elementary and secondary teachers in public schools and in schools of a semi-public nature are given, but no information is presented concerning qualifications for special teachers, i.e., those engaged in crafts work, in vocational training, or in other non-academic activities, and for European teachers serving on temporary certificates. Detailed studies of teacher training in certain European countries, notably in France, Germany, and Sweden, are already available, as are similar studies for the American states included in this investigation. A more thorough inquiry into teacher status in some or all of the foreign countries included in the present study would doubtless produce results of value both to American and European educators. But in this study it was only possible, and it also appeared sufficient, to trace in rather broad outline existing requirements and current practices in these countries, showing where these differ from, are inferior or superior to, similar conditions in the indefinite tenure states of the United States.

TRAINING OF TEACHERS

American states having indefinite tenure statutes maintain, on the whole, less adequate safeguards for the teaching profession and for children in the schools in the form of scholastic requirements for entering the field than do the European countries included in this study. Table XVI shows the minimum number of college years of study required for teaching on the various school levels in the American states as of June 1932. Comparable data for the several foreign countries comprise the major part of this section on teacher training. Data for both this country and Europe represent only general requirements prevailing in large governmental units which must be met by new regular teachers.

Teacher Tenure in America and in Europe

Minimum prerequisites for teaching may not in some cases truthfully represent the qualifications of teachers in the field; still, it cannot be denied that the very existence of low requirements constitutes a continual threat to any school system under which they operate. All facts presented and comparisons made in this and later sections apply to teachers of either the elementary or secondary level. It is admitted that the school divisions of European countries are not exactly equivalent to the main American

TABLE XVI

Minimum Training Requirements for Teaching in Terms of College Years Operating in States Having Indefinite Tenure Laws, June 1932[1]

State	School Levels				
	Rural and Ungraded	Kindergarten	Elementary	Junior H. S.	Senior H. S
California	--	4	4[2]	4	5
Colorado	--	--	2	--	4
District of Columbia	--	--	3	3	4
Illinois	--	1	1	--	2
Indiana	--	2	2	3	4
Louisiana	--	--	1½	1½	4
Maryland	--	--	3	--	4
Massachusetts	--	--	--	--	4[3]
Minnesota	1	Diploma (Time not stated)	2	4	4
New Jersey	--	2	3	4	4
New York	1	2	2	4	4
Oregon	--	2	2	2	4
Wisconsin	1	--	2	--	4

[1] The data given were received directly from the certification bureaus of the respective state departments represented, except in the case of requirements which had not changed since 1927, at which time the United States Bureau of Education issued its Bulletin No. 19, "State Laws and Regulations Governing Teachers' Certificates."

[2] High school graduation and a county examination are really the lowest requirements for elementary teachers in California, but extremely few teachers enter by this route.

[3] For state-aided high schools only (of which there were about 40 in 1926). Certification of all other Massachusetts teachers is entirely a local matter.

ones, i.e., elementary, junior high, and senior high; however, there appears to be sufficient similarity to warrant guarded comparisons.

Elementary Teachers

Although American teachers in indefinite tenure states, as a group, have to meet less stringent requirements than those of the six European countries under consideration, the difference does not seem to exist on the elementary level. According to Table XVI, the range in college years required in the American states is 0 to 4; a similar range exists in the foreign countries. It is probable that the American states have a slight advantage in point of quantity alone; but, if so, the difference is too small to merit consideration. Quality of training, at least as far as this can be assumed by the type of institution in which instruction is given, is very nearly the same in both cases. The American elementary teacher receives her training either in a normal school or in the education department of some college or university; similarly, the European teacher, except in Italy, receives specialized training in either a normal school or university. High school graduation is a prerequisite for beginning training for elementary work in the United States and the equivalent, or more than this, is required in European countries which do not include normal schools in their secondary programs. Examinations for certificates are required more frequently by the European countries than by the American states; yet there are some states, e.g., Illinois and Oregon, that require examinations when only minimum qualifications are submitted. A brief exposition of the lowest requirements in the American states and of general conditions abroad will clarify the entire situation.

In five American states, California, Massachusetts, Minnesota, New York, and Wisconsin, legal certificates are still obtainable on the basis of very meager educational training. California provides for certification of elementary teachers solely on proof of high school graduation and a county examination; but the number now issued on this basis, as Cubberley[7] has pointed out, is negligible. Minnesota, New York, and Wisconsin grant certificates to candidates who have completed one year of college work, which permit them to teach in rural or ungraded schools, and Massachusetts has no legal scholarship prerequisite for elementary teachers, certification being left entirely to local authorities. Despite this absence of requirements, Cook[8] says that, according to authoritative statements, relatively few teachers are employed in the state who have not completed a standard normal course.

[7] Cubberley, E. P., *State School Administration*, pp. 622, 632.
[8] Cook, Katherine M., *State Laws and Regulations Governing Teachers' Certificates*, p. 14.

The lowest requirements prevailing in the European countries maintain in Italy and Sweden, where examinations for elementary teaching certificates may be taken at the end of twelve and ten years of formal schooling, respectively. Italian teaching candidates enter upon a seven-year period of training[9] immediately after completing the universal five-year elementary curriculum. The institutions in which they are instructed are a part of the secondary school system[10] and offer practically the same curricula; the amount of professional training given is extremely small. Successful negotiation of a comprehensive examination, covering the last three years of the seven-year course, is the minimum qualification for competing for elementary teaching positions.[11] In Sweden, regular elementary teachers, i.e., those in the upper four years of the six-year elementary school, must have passed a prescribed examination, the *folkskollärareexamen*,[12] which ordinarily is taken at the close of a four-year normal school course. Entrance to normal school is by examination based on work equivalent to the curriculum of the six-year elementary school and the minimum age requirement is seventeen. Due to keen competition, many students use the interim between completion of elementary school and beginning of normal school training for study in intermediate and secondary schools. In 1927 only 37 per cent of the beginning students in normal schools had had no preliminary training beyond the elementary school.[13] Some few candidates qualify for the required examination by completing a secondary school course and a one-year course in a normal school.[14] Teachers in the first two years of the Swedish elementary school may qualify for their work by taking a two-year course in a primary normal school and a special examination;[15] but there is a question as to whether they can gain permanent status.

Three European countries, England and Wales, France, and Norway, require the general equivalent of two American college years of study. Of this group, England and Wales employ practices most similar to those in vogue in the American states. A large

[9] Article 53, *Bollettino Ufficiale*, p. 812, July 7, 1923.
[10] Kandel, I. L., *Comparative Education*, p. 588.
[11] *Ibid.*, pp. 589-90.
[12] Borgeson, Frithiof Carl, *The Administration of Elementary and Secondary Education in Sweden*, p. 33.
[13] Kilander, Holger F., *Science Education in the Secondary Schools of Sweden*, p. 18.
[14] Educational Pamphlets, No. 81, p. 193, Board of Education, England.
[15] Borgeson, *op. cit.*, p. 35.

majority of elementary teachers in England and Wales receive their instruction in special training colleges maintained by private denominational or local educational authorities and the others are trained in university training departments, where they take regular university work during the first three years and specialized training in pedagogy during the fourth. Practically all of the students in training colleges take the regular two-year course, but some few take three- or four-year courses. Entrance to a training college is open only to students who have passed an examination approved by the Board of Education,[16] the central authority for education in England and Wales, covering work equal to a full high school course in the United States. The Board's certificate, now usually obtained by successfully passing an examination upon completing a training course, is a prerequisite for teaching.[17]

As a rule, elementary teachers in France are trained in normal schools (*écoles normales*), which commonly provide only a three-year course. Admission to such schools is open to teaching candidates who have completed a higher elementary school course, leading to the *brevet élémentaire*, and who have passed a competitive entrance examination.[18] Normal school students who pass satisfactorily the final examination are granted the title of *brevet supérieur*, which may be regarded as certification to teach.

To qualify for a permanent appointment in the upper grades of the seven-year elementary school in Norway, a teacher must pass either a regular or special normal school examination, the former coming at the close of a four-year normal school course and the latter at the end of a special course, of not less than two years in length, open only to graduates of secondary schools.[19] The lowest requirement for entrance to the four-year normal school course is successful completion of the elementary school and six months of continuation school work, but practically all entrants have been through the middle school (*middelskole*)[20] or some type of continuation school.[21] Teachers in the lower division of the ele-

[16] Statutory Rules and Orders, 1926, No. 954, p. 3.
[17] Uncertificated teachers are still employed in some areas, but this practice is fast disappearing.
[18] Kandel, I. L., *French Elementary Schools*, p. 17.
[19] *Skolväsendet I Tio Länder*, p. 263 (Lov, June 6, 1930).
[20] The middle school is the first three years of the six-year secondary school period. It is followed by the *Gymnasium*, also three years in length, in which courses are mostly of college grade.
[21] *Skolväsendet I Tio Länder*, p. 261.

mentary school, i.e., the first, second, and third years, may not have to meet as high requirements as those outlined, but proof of this could not be obtained.

Germany stands considerably above the other European countries in the matter of training requirements for elementary teachers and also surpasses all the American states, unless it be California. Variations exist among the several German states; yet, generally speaking, training is carried on in all of them in universities or in institutions of university rank and the lowest requirement is two years of professional study, with the possible exception of Württemberg. Entrance to training institutions is contingent upon completion of a secondary school, which means that beginning students are as far advanced, at least from an academic standpoint, as are students in American colleges at the end of their sophomore year. With regard to the length of the professional preparation period in the several states, Alexander says:

> The training lasts three years in Saxony, Thuringia, Hamburg, Brunswick, Anhalt, and Lippe; and two years in Prussia, Baden, Hesse, Mecklenburg, Oldenburg, and Waldeck.[22]

Secondary Teachers

As has already been intimated, training requirements for secondary teachers are considerably higher in the six European countries than in the several American states. The prevailing requirement in the indefinite tenure states or four years of college study and the range is from one and one-half to approximately six. In the foreign countries no single number of years predominates, but the range, reckoned on the basis of American college years, is approximately four to nine.[23] Although the general difference in requirements may be accounted for in part by the greater scope of European secondary schools and their consequent need for more highly trained teachers, it also seems to be partially due to the maintenance by the European countries of a planned policy of protection of secondary school interests through high training requirements for secondary teachers. Even on the middle school level, which is roughly comparable to the American junior high school, the lowest requirement for teachers seems to be the

---

[22] Alexander, Thomas, *The Training of Elementary Teachers in Germany*, p. 31.

[23] "American college years" presuppose prior completion of the equivalent of the American secondary school curriculum.

equivalent of five American college years of study. As concerns the quality of training, the American teacher probably has the advantage from the standpoint of techniques and methods and the European teacher excels in academic training. The former receives his training in a normal school, a college, or a university; the latter is invariably trained in a university or institution of university rank.

The lowest requirements prevailing in any of the American states are found in Illinois, Louisiana, Oregon, and Indiana. Two years of college study and an examination are sufficient for senior high school teaching in Illinois; and for teaching on the junior high school level in the other three states, only one and one-half, two, and three years, respectively, are required. Comparison of these figures with the lowest ones for the foreign countries, i.e., those for England and Wales and for Italy, also those for the middle schools of Norway and Sweden, bring out one feature of the superiority of the European countries.

In England and Wales, no legal prescriptions exist for either the academic or professional training of secondary teachers or for their certification, but in practice the qualification for secondary teaching has been a university degree.[24] Students in any of the universities of England may pursue either an honors course or a pass, or ordinary, course. Kandel[25] says that the honors degree represents specialization comparable to that required for the Master of Arts if not the Doctor of Philosophy degree in an American university. The pass course is more nearly equivalent to a four-year college course in the United States. Students taking a pass course may give their last year over to professional preparation, but almost all secondary teaching candidates obtain their pedagogical training through a one-year postgraduate course, combining theory and practice, taken in the education department of a university. Secondary teachers in Italy have to take courses which may range from three to six or seven years in length, the modal period being four years,[26] and which are very nearly altogether of an academic nature. Certification to teach is based entirely on the results of state examinations and not on evidence of courses completed. The teaching candidate must, however, have

[24] *Yearbook of Education, 1932*, p. 276.
[25] Kandel, I. L., *Comparative Education*, p. 834.
[26] *Yearbook of Education, 1932*, pp. 866, 873; Kandel, I. L., *Comparative Education*, p. 850.

Teacher Tenure in America and in Europe 123

very definite educational qualifications in order to be allowed to take any one of the several examinations.

France and Germany rank in the middle of the European countries as regards training required of secondary teachers. Two years of university training or its equivalent is now considered to be the minimum qualification in France.[27] The teacher who secures his two years of instruction in a university is granted the degree of *licence* and by at least two years of further study and successful negotiation of a competitive examination of the highest level, may attain the title of *agrégé*. This title represents training at least equal in length and intensity to that evidenced by the American Doctor of Philosophy degree. It is a prerequisite for appointment to a full professorship in a *lycée*,[28] and, according to McMurry,[29] is the real goal of all secondary teachers. The training of French secondary teachers is predominantly academic in character; methods and techniques play a very small part in it.

All secondary teachers of Prussia, which may be taken as fairly representative of Germany, must have completed eight semesters, or four years, of university study and two additional years of practical training before becoming eligible for an appointment carrying a salary.[30] Alexander[31] says that for Prussian secondary teachers the minimum length of time spent in preparation, including time spent preparing for the final examination at the university (*Staatsexamen*) and in practical work, is six and one-half to seven years; and the average, eight and one-half to nine years. Consequently, secondary teachers of Prussia are perhaps better qualified than teachers of similar rank in any other country or governmental unit of the world.

Regular teachers of academic, or theoretical subjects, in the secondary schools of Norway and Sweden rank at the top of the countries and states included in this study as far as academic training is concerned. Such teachers, with the exception of some middle school (*realskole*) teachers in Norway,[32] are trained in universities and are divided into two ranks, viz., *lektorer* and

---

[27] Richard, C., *L'Enseignement en France*, pp. 64, 67.
[28] Décret 10 avril, 1852, Article 6; Dion, L., *Recueil Complet de la Législation de l'Enseignement Secondaire*, p. 206.
[29] McMurry, Ruth E., Mueller, Max, and Alexander, Thomas, *Modern Foreign Languages in France and Germany*, p. 84.
[30] *Ibid.*, pp. 370, 384.
[31] *Ibid.*, p. 171.
[32] This minority group receive their training in normal schools.

adjunkter, the former being the higher. Teaching candidates at the University of Oslo, in Norway, take either a four- or a seven-year course, both of which are terminated by final university examinations (*embedsekamener*).[33] After completing one of these courses, the candidate must take a semester of professional training in the pedagogical seminary, which is under the direct control of the Department of Church and Education.[34] In Sweden the university degree of "Master of Philosophy," which normally requires five years of study, is the prerequisite for the rank of *adjunkt*; and approximately nine years of university study and three university degrees, the highest that of Doctor of Philosophy, are required for the rank of *lektor*.[35] Teaching on the *Gymnasium* level in both countries is done entirely by *lektorer*, while both *lektorer* and *adjunkter* teach in the middle school. Loftfield[36] says that the aim in Norway is to have all secondary teachers holders of the *lektor* degree.

APPOINTMENTS, PROBATIONARY PERIODS, AND TRANSFERS

Largely due to the high degree of centralized control of education existing in the European countries, with the exception of England and Wales, procedures for appointment of teachers and regulations concerning probation and transfers are more uniform and, in the main, appear to be more efficient than those found in the American states. Local education authorities in some of the foreign countries select and appoint teachers, usually of elementary rank only; but this is commonly done under the close supervision of central educational authorities. Competitive examinations also play a more important rôle in the appointment of European teachers than is the case with American teachers. Probationary periods are more flexible, i.e., are more variable in length, abroad than in this country and often are longer. Furthermore, provision is made in some European countries for retention of teachers who have served periods of probation without granting them permanent rank. And, finally, the situation in the foreign countries is more conducive to the making of transfers than is that of the American states.

[33] *Rundskrivelse fra Kirke—og Undervisningsdepartementet*, pp. 1-2.
[34] Loftfield, Gabriel E., *Secondary Education in Norway*, pp. 86-89.
[35] Board of Education, *op. cit.*, pp. 193-94.
[36] Loftfield, Gabriel E., *Secondary Education in Norway*, p. 79.

Appointments

Selection and appointment of teachers in the American states comprise a local problem which is handled entirely by local administrative officers and their boards of education. In striking contrast to this are the practices of the European countries, where central authorities[37] appoint all of the teachers in some countries and a considerable percentage of the total in others. Elementary teachers are appointed by local authorities[38] in England and Wales, in Norway, and in Sweden and by central authorities in France, Italy, and Prussia. Secondary teachers are appointed by central authorities in all countries except England and Wales. Appointments are in general to specific positions rather than to service in a given administrative unit.

Some elementary teaching positions in England and Wales are filled by open competition after advertisement of the vacancies. Public announcement of all school vacancies must be made in Norway, with complete details specified; and in Sweden all vacancies must be advertised in the official state paper and are usually advertised in school magazines and daily papers as well. Appointments made by local boards of control in Norway are subject to approval by a central authority, the local school director (*overtilsynet: skoldirektören*), and it is probable that a similar requirement exists in Sweden.

Elementary teachers in France are appointed to probationary positions by the primary inspectors, who are state officials not subordinate to any local authorities,[39] and to permanent places by the prefects in the ninety departments, or governmental divisions of the country, who act upon the recommendations of academy inspectors.[40] Appointment of elementary teachers in Germany and assignment of duties to them is thus explained by Alexander:[41]

As it exists today the state has the right of appointment while, to a certain degree, the choice of the individual is left to the community, but, as the state

---

[37] "Central authority" as used in this chapter refers to a ministry or department of education or to some representative of such a body, acting as head of a reasonably large administrative unit.
[38] "Local authority" in this chapter refers to any local governing body or official.
[39] Kandel, I. L., *French Elementary Schools*, pp. 8, 20.
[40] Loi du octobre 1886, article 27; Décret organique (18 janvier 1887), article 21; Circulaire ou instruction ministérielle 10 juillet 1906; Soleil, Joseph, *Le Livre des Instituteurs*, p. 185.
[41] Alexander, *op. cit.*, pp. 288, 290.

participates more and more in bearing school costs, it takes greater authority in the selection of teachers.

In the certificate of appointment the school corporation or unit is indicated but not the school position, since another position may be assigned the teacher against his will. The appointment is provisional. . . . (*supra*[41])

In Italy appointments to all elementary teaching positions are made either by the regional superintendents of public education (*provveditore agli studi*) or by the councils of autonomous communities. Vacancies are advertised each year by these authorities and certificated teachers are chosen to fill them by means of a competitive examination, preference being shown those who make the highest scores.[42]

Although secondary teachers in European countries are appointed by central authorities in all cases except in England and Wales, the procedures used by the several countries vary considerably. Candidates for positions in England and Wales, where local authorities have complete charge, and in Italy, where appointment is by a decree of the Ministry of Education,[43] must pass a competitive examination. The ranks made by Italian competitors determine who will be selected for existing vacancies and who will be given the diploma of eligibility, which entitles its holders to teach in private schools.[44]

According to legal statute, the Minister of Education in France, by delegation of the President of the Republic, appoints the professors and functionaries of secondary education.[45] This absolute power is in reality exercised only in a nominal sense, for the Minister actually acts upon the suggestions of the highest educational officials (the *rectors*) in the large governmental units (the *academies*). State educational authorities appoint all secondary teachers in Prussia, making their selections for permanent positions from an eligibility list (*Anwärterliste*) prepared by the Ministry of Education with the aid of provincial, or sectional school boards.[46] Appointment of all permanent secondary teachers in Norway[47] and of secondary teachers in general in Sweden[48] is a

---

[42] Kandel, I. L., *Comparative Education*, pp. 590-91.

[43] Decree of September 30, 1922, No. 1290. Letter from T. Jaeckel, American Consul General, Rome, Italy, March 10, 1932.

[44] Kandel, I. L., *Comparative Education*, p. 850.

[45] Décret 9 mars 1852, mod. par la loi du mars 1873. Dion, L., *Recueil Complet de la Législation de l'Enseignement Secondaire*, p. 99.

[46] Kandel, I. L., *Comparative Education*, p. 847.

[47] *De Høiere Almenskoler*, Par. 33, p. 15.

[48] For details concerning appointment procedures, see Borgeson, *op. cit.*, pp. 157-61.

power reserved to the respective Kings of these two countries. Communal secondary schools in Norway make their own appointments, subject, however, to the approval of central authorities.

Probationary Requirements and Practices

Legal prescriptions regarding probation in the European countries establish no higher requirements for attainment of permanent status than exist in the American states. As a matter of fact, foreign regulations may be termed lower than those of this country, for England and Wales require no period of trial service of secondary teachers and a similar condition holds for elementary teachers in Norway and Sweden. But due to a number of other factors, namely, certain personnel regulations and precedents and very high competition for positions, it is much more difficult for European teachers to acquire permanent status than for American teachers. Tenure accrues in all or practically all of the American states as a natural result of the completion of fixed periods of probationary service. In the European countries, taken as a whole, permanent status can be gained only through direct action of educational authorities and this often does not follow immediately the end of probation. During the variable interims, teachers are frequently employed as substitutes or as regular teachers with non-permanent rank. Examinations and supervision or inspection are emphasized much more in the administration of probationary service by the European countries, generally speaking, than by the American states.

The most common probationary requirement in the American states is three years of service and the range is one to five (pages 28 f., 32). These facts are similar to corresponding data for the European countries, where no one length of period predominates and where the ranges are from one to five years on the elementary level and from one to three on the secondary. But general figures do not tell the whole story. For the American states it has been told in sufficient detail in other chapters of this study; therefore, forthcoming detailed facts have to do only with the European countries.

European elementary teachers, even in Norway and Sweden where probationary periods are not required by law, have had considerable experience before gaining permanent status. Norwegian elementary teachers usually proceed to permanent rank through substitute and temporary service, in which capacities they spend several years. In England and Wales, newly-trained teachers are on probation their first year in the field, this being regarded as an extra year of training.[49] The Board of Education merely requires such a period and leaves to the County Councils the matter of working out specific provisions. The London County Council, for instance, has a rule which states that a probationary appointment shall be confirmed at the end of the first year of service if the probationer has been rated satisfactory; but if not confirmed, the teacher may continue on trial up to the end of the third year.[50] Probationers in France (*instituteurs stagiaires*) must complete two years of service in public elementary schools before becoming eligible for appointment as permanent teachers (*instituteurs titulaires*).[51] Some French elementary teachers are on probation longer than two years and all must have the certificate of pedagogical efficiency (*certificat d'aptitude pédagogique*), obtained by passing a practical examination, before becoming eligible for permanent appointment.[52] A pedagogical, or practical examination (*Zweite Lehrer Prüfung*) is also required of German elementary teachers; it is taken after completing two and before finishing five years of probationary service.[53] The new elementary teacher appointee in Italy must serve three years as a probationer (*maestro straordinario*),[54] during which time he must complete twenty-five months of actual teaching. If this is not done, the trial period is extended until the twenty-five months are completed, provided this is accomplished within four years from the date of original appointment.[55]

Secondary teachers in the foreign countries, as a group, have to meet as stringent probationary requirements as do elementary teachers. England and Wales are the only countries where trial service of some kind is not a prerequisite for the acquirement of permanent status. In Italy, secondary teachers have to meet the same conditions as those of elementary rank, viz., three years of

[49] Wilson, J. Dover (Ed.), *The Schools of England*, p. 220.
[50] Handbook Containing General Information with Reference to Teachers, Instructors and Instructresses in London Public Elementary Schools, 1928, pp. 18-19.
[51] Loi du 30 octobre 1886, article 23, mod. 3 août 1926; Soleil, Joseph, *op. cit.*, p. 179.
[52] Loi du 30 octobre 1886, article 23, mod. 6 octobre 1919; Soleil, *Ibid.*
[53] Kandel, I. L. and Alexander, Thomas (Translators), *The Reorganization of Education in Prussia*, p. xxvi.
[54] Article 131, *Testo Unico*, p. 51.
[55] Article 313, *Regolamento Generale*, p. 102.

trial service, during which period they are known as extraordinary professors (*professori straordinari*).[56] Probationary service in France ranges from one to three years; and additional requirements for a full professorship in a *lycée* (state supported and controlled secondary school) are that the candidate be twenty-five years of age and have five years of service in public education to his credit.[57] The German secondary teacher, upon completing his university course, is assigned to a public school for two years of professional training and study terminating with the pedagogical examination (*Padagogische Prüfung*). There follows then several years of service in temporary positions. Alexander[58] states that the normal age for final appointment of secondary teachers seems to be thirty-two to thirty-three years and that some are over forty or fifty. In the words of this authority,

The terrific pressure under which the German secondary school teachers labor for final appointment is something unknown to America.[59]

Two years of probation must be satisfactorily completed by secondary teachers in Norway before they become eligible for permanent appointment;[60] and in Sweden such teachers have to serve a probationary year without pay, in specially selected State Higher Public Secondary Schools, and to obtain in addition two years of practical teaching experience.[61]

Temporary or non-permanent positions, other than those of the probationary type, apparently exist in all the European countries except England and Wales. Evidence already adduced establishes this condition for both elementary and secondary teachers of France and Germany, and it also holds for secondary teachers of Italy. In Norway one-third of all full-time teaching positions in city elementary schools must be of the temporary type; teachers are appointed to them *på opsigelse*, that is, with the understanding that they may be dismissed at any time on three months' notice.[62] In rural elementary schools one-third of all positions in the upper elementary grades and one-half of those in the lower division may be of temporary character.[63] The minimum number

[56] Kandel, I. L., *Comparative Education*, pp. 851-52.
[57] Décret 26 novembre 1875, article 2; Dion, L., *op. cit.*, p. 206.
[58] McMurry, Mueller, and Alexander, *op. cit.*, pp. 464, 471.
[59] *Ibid.*, p. 463.
[60] *De Høiere Almenskoler*, *op. cit.*
[61] Board of Education, England, *op. cit.*, p. 194.
[62] *Lov om Folkeskolen I Kjøpstedene*, Par. 30, p. 13.
[63] *Lov om Folkeskolen Paa Landet*, Par. 29, p. 16.

of permanent (*ordinaire*) positions each type of school in Sweden must maintain is fixed by law. For instance, each elementary school must have one permanent teacher (*supra*[61]). Borgeson[64] states that from 15 to 20 per cent of all elementary and secondary teachers are not on regular appointment, the minimum of permanent teachers being used for economic reasons. The lengths of time spent in temporary (*icke-ordinaire*) positions by secondary teachers are ordinarily three to six years for *lektorer* and ten years for *adjunkter*. In practice, secondary teachers do not receive permanent appointment until they are thirty to thirty-five years of age.

Transfers

European school systems have an advantage over the American indefinite tenure states in the matter of transfers, owing to their centralized administrative organizations. As was shown in Chapter V, transfers within local systems in the American states may present real difficulties and risks. And transfers among local systems are out of the question, since this would mean loss of accrued tenure protection by the teachers involved. The European situation is in theory much more favorable to the effecting of transfers, and in reality it appears to facilitate shifts of assignment appreciably.

No information with regard to this point was obtained for England and Wales, and for France the only fact established was that the law provides for the assignment of married teachers to the same department, or district, and to the same community. Twenty-five per cent of the elementary vacancies arising annually in each department are reserved for transfers of married teachers.[65] Public school teachers in the state-supported schools of Germany may be transferred upon request or when it appears best for the service; but city school teachers, i.e., those in state-aided schools, cannot be transferred out of the localities in which they received appointment. Secondary probationers in Italy may be transferred without any loss of credit for time already served.[66] If unsatisfactory in their new positions, they are returned to the districts where first appointed and there resume probationary ser-

---

[64] Borgeson, *op. cit.*, p. 163.
[65] Loi du décembre 1921; Soleil, *op. cit.*, p. 189.
[66] Article 6 of the Royal Decree of May 6, 1923, No. 1054; *Bollettino Ufficiale*, Vol. 1, No. 23, p. 1807.

vice as though the transfers had not been made.[67] Transfers are also possible in Norway, and presumably in Sweden, but no specific data were obtained concerning procedures.

TENURE AND DISCIPLINARY REGULATIONS AND PRACTICES

Most outstanding of the differences existing between the European countries and the American states as regards tenure, specifically, are that in several of the foreign countries some or all educational employees are really civil servants and in England and Wales indefinite tenure has no authority other than that of precedent. Disciplinary provisions vary principally in that those of the foreign countries are more elaborate than those of the American states. Little evidence could be obtained concerning the actual results of indefinite tenure in the European countries; nevertheless, it appears certain that foreign teachers with permanent status enjoy a high degree of security, and this means that it is likely that the problem of dismissal presents as many difficulties abroad as in this country.

Tenure

Even though indefinite tenure has no legal sanction in England and Wales, it maintains universally in practice, both school workers and the public accepting it as a matter of course. Selby-Bigge[68] states that tenure of teachers is continuous after "recognition" (permanent appointment) has been granted; and the handbooks of information issued by the several County Councils commonly refer to teachers as being probationary or permanent employees. All regular public school teachers in France, Germany,[69] and Sweden and all secondary teachers in Norway are civil servants, as well as members of a well-established profession, and as such have indefinite tenure. Protected tenure may have existed longest in Sweden, for all state employees there have had life tenure since the seventeenth century.[70] Elementary teachers in Norway are communal officials, but, like the secondary teachers,

[67] Article 16 of the Royal Decree of November 27, 1924; *Bollettino Ufficiale*, No. 15, p. 2036, April 14, 1925.
[68] Selby-Bigge, Sir Lewis A., *The Board of Education*, p. 272.
[69] Oktavec, Frank L., *The Professional Education of Special Men Teachers of Physical Education in Prussia*, p. 102.
[70] Borgeson, *op. cit.*, p. 161.

they are protected in their positions. To the existence of indefinite tenure, Loftfield[71] attributes the high social standing of secondary teachers in Norway:

> A fundamental reason for the high social standing of the Norwegian teacher is his life tenure of position. He considers such tenure to be a matter of course, since he is educated and trained for a specific purpose largely at the expense of the state.[72]

Italian education law states that the appointment of elementary teachers "acquires character of stability" after completion of the three-year probationary period[72] and that secondary teachers advance to the rank of ordinary professors (*professori ordinari*), a permanent rank, upon completing their trial service.[73]

Both Borgeson[74] and Kilander[75] have discussed the effects of indefinite tenure in Sweden. They point out that it may be credited with partial responsibility for the highly professional attitude teachers manifest toward their work; but that it also gives a composure which tempts teachers to resign themselves to existing educational practices. The ease (*arbetsro*) which the Swedish teacher shows in his work is said to be unknown to teachers in the United States, even in those states which have protected tenure.[76]

Difficult and undesirable administrative situations occasionally develop in Sweden as a result of the fact that secondary teachers may lay claim to their original posts, to which they were specifically appointed, at any time during their life, even after accepting appointments outside the school field. Borgeson[77] tells of one such case which the Royal Board, the central authority for education, was attempting to solve in 1926. Due to the transfer of two *lektorer* and the subsequent desire of one of them to return to his original position, a school was in danger of having two or three *lektorer* in history and geography and no teachers of such rank in physics and chemistry. Such an outcome would have given the school several *lektorer* in a subject field in which comparable schools have only one; and, furthermore, it would have given the school only *adjunkter* in an important science field. Another

[71] Loftfield, *op. cit.*, p. 97.
[72] Article 131, *op. cit.*
[73] Article 6, *op. cit.*
[74] Borgeson, *op. cit.*, p. 161.
[75] Kilander, *op. cit.*, pp. 18-19.
[76] Borgeson, *op. cit.*, p. 161.
[77] *Ibid.*, p. 162.

case cited by the same authority was that of a nervous teacher who could not maintain discipline.[78] He was removed from his position for one year by the Royal Board, but resumed his duties at the end of this time over the protests of the head of the school. Without an act of Parliament, no permanent teacher can be removed from the teaching service as long as he meets his classes.

Discipline

In this study, all data pertaining to disciplinary regulations in the European countries indicate a marked similarity to provisions existent in the American states, except where differences arise naturally from the practice of centralized administration in Europe. In cases where details were available, it was found that provision is made for charges, for a hearing or investigation, for imposition of a penalty, and for an appeal where the ruling authority is of lesser rank than the highest in the country. The greatest differences appear in connection with scales of penalties, those of foreign countries being more elaborate. Dismissal is practically the only penalty imposed in the American states, but in several of the European countries penalties graduated in degree of severity are imposed.

England and Wales have no laws concerning discipline of teachers, save that the power of removal is reserved to local authorities.[79] The several County Councils have set up their own provisions for disciplining teachers. For example, the London County Council has drawn up rules for the handling of all complaints against teachers, which provide, in the case of serious charges, for inquiries by school officials, for hearings at which the accused teachers may defend themselves in person or through witnesses, and for final decisions, except when recourse to law courts is taken.[80] As just implied, appeal to the law courts is open to teachers who become the subjects of disciplinary action.

An interesting feature of tenure disputes in England and Wales is that the National Union of Teachers, a professional organization composed largely of elementary teachers, through its Tenure Committee, furnishes the teachers involved legal and advisory aid. The 1930 report[81] of the Committee calls attention to the com-

[78] *Ibid.*, pp. 162-63.
[79] Section 148, Education Act of 1921.
[80] Handbook, *op. cit.*, pp. 60-62.
[81] *National Union of Teachers: Report for 1930*, pp. lxvii-lxix.

plexity of the tenure problem and classifies the types of cases that it has to consider, this classification being as follows: individual advice cases; individual tenure cases; difficulties connected with reorganization; group cases, etc., such as dismissal at sixty years of age; and secondary school cases. During 1930 the Committee met fourteen times and considered 1,117 cases; in addition, it gave advice on 693 other cases.

Discipline of Prussian teachers, in addition to dismissal from the service, may take three forms: (1) warning, (2) proof, or censure (*Verweis*), and (3) monetary fine.[82] Removal may be effected either by transfer to another school without change of rank or by complete dismissal from the service. Charges upon which a teacher may be permanently dismissed are: (1) any offense as an official of the State;[83] and (2) offenses of a private nature which affect adversely his occupational worth.

In the four remaining foreign countries, i.e., France, Italy, Norway, and Sweden, somewhat different disciplinary regulations hold for elementary and secondary teachers. This is doubtless attributable to the fact that the two groups of teachers are clearly separated from each other in the several countries. In Norway and Sweden this separation indicates a partially different type of control of teacher personnel on the two levels, local authorities having more power in the case of elementary teachers.

Grounds for dismissal of elementary teachers in Norway are incompetency, incapacity, and improper conduct in the school or in private life;[84] and almost identical grounds, with the addition of negligence of duty, apply in Sweden.[85] Temporary suspension seems to be available as a disciplinary measure in the latter country and may be used in the former pending the outcome of cases involving serious offenses. Local boards of education in Norway exercise disciplinary authority; they act in agreement with district school directors, after allowing accused teachers an opportunity to defend themselves. The district administrative body of the Swedish state church, the Chapter, acts as an administrative tribunal to pass on all disciplinary action concerning elementary teachers in Sweden; and appeal to higher courts is allowed. The difficulty of removal of Swedish teachers in general has been

---

[82] Kühn, Walter, *Schulrecht in Preussen*, pp. 363-64, 368.
[83] Law of July 21, 1852; Kühn, *op. cit.*, p. 368.
[84] *Lov om Folkeskolen I Kjøpstedene*, Par. 34, pp. 14-15.
[85] Borgeson, *op. cit.*, p. 163.

pointed out by Borgeson, and commented upon as follows:

> It is very unusual for any elementary or secondary school teacher actually to be dismissed after he has received permanent appointment—in fact, it is almost impossible. Teachers enter the profession with the intention of remaining in it for life, and as a rule have had a high standing in the community.[86]

Information obtained for France and Italy was in greater detail than that for any of the other foreign countries. Rigid codes of discipline, similar in general features, prevail in the two countries. In Italy, the legal grounds for disciplinary action against elementary teachers are: (1) habitual negligence, (2) transgression or violation of duties imposed by law or school rules, (3) personal misconduct, and (4) promotion of principles contrary to morality and state politics.[87] Inefficiency of service is partially defined by school law, which states that a teacher may be dismissed for such cause if reports concerning the last three years show clearly that he is inefficient, particular emphasis being placed on the number of students promoted; or if the teacher has not given at least ten months of satisfactory service during the last four years.[88]

Grounds for dismissal only, applying to all functionaries, were found in the case of France: (1) misconduct, and (2) "necessity of service."[89] The former includes incompetency as well as unbecoming conduct and the latter can be invoked only in emergencies, displaced functionaries then being sent to equivalent posts. Accused elementary teachers in both countries must be notified of disciplinary proceedings against them and given an opportunity to defend themselves; and as a further safeguard to such teachers in France, they are guaranteed access to their complete official records. Punishments established by law for elementary teachers of France are: (1) reprimand, (2) censure, (3) revocation, and (4) interdiction, either temporary or permanent.[90] Admonition and reproach are also mentioned in the law, but these penalties are not disciplinary measures.[91] Revocation deprives the teacher of only the right to teach in public schools, while interdiction forbids one to teach either in public or private schools.

[86] *Ibid.*   [87] Article 150, *Testo Unico*, p. 58.
[88] Article 321, *Regolamento Generale*, p. 105.
[89] Loi du octobre 1886, article 29; Soleil, *op. cit.*, p. 189.
[90] Loi du 30 octobre 1886, articles 31 and 32; Lantenois, A., *Ce que l'Instituteur doit Savoir*, p. 511.
[91] Conseil d'Etat, 30 mars 1906, 3 mai 1912. . . . *Journal Officiel*, 11 mars 1925; Lantenois, *op. cit.*

Legal penalties in Italy are similar to those just cited for France, but also include provision for suspension of salary up to a limit of ten days and for suspension from service without pay for a maximum of six months.[92] Central authorities impose the penalties in both countries, except in autonomous Italian communities, where the mayors act. Teachers in the two countries may appeal from adverse decisions by lower educational authorities to higher authorities, either educational or governmental.

The higher central authorities in the four countries under consideration have almost complete control of the discipline of secondary teachers within their borders. In Norway, dismissals are effected by the Ministry of Education, at the instance of local school boards, for incompetency, incapacity to discharge duties, or for improper personal conduct.[93] Two-thirds of a local board must agree before a petition can be forwarded to the Ministry asking for removal of a teacher. Disciplinary matters are handled by the Royal Board (educational) and the legislative body of the Swedish Government, the penalties inflicted being temporary suspension and dismissal. In principle, at least, discipline of secondary teachers in France is in the hands of the Minister of Education;[94] but, in practice, lower central authorities act and the Minister merely supervises. He must approve all dismissals from service; and he has the right of pronouncing independently reprimand and censure penalties, and of suspending teachers.[95] Causes for action and procedures are much the same as in the case of elementary teachers. Italian secondary teachers may suffer admonishment, censure, and suspension from salary up to one month for minor offenses; for grave insubordination, habitual irregularities of conduct, and facts compromising the honor and dignity of teachers, they may be suspended from salary and office up to a maximum of one year or may be permanently removed with or without loss of rights to pensions and allowances.[96] Local authorities may suspend teachers in emergencies, notifying the Minister immediately of such action.[97] Appeals from some decisions are allowed and presumably from all.

[92] Article 150, *Testo Unico*, pp. 58-59.
[93] *De Høiere Almenskoler*, Par. 71, p. 24.
[94] Loi du 30 octobre, article 31; Soleil, *op. cit.*, p. 79.
[95] Loi du février 1880, articles 13 and 15; Dion, *op. cit.*, pp. 627-28.
[96] Articles 22 and 23 of the Royal Decree of May 6, 1923, No. 1054; *Bollettino Ufficiale*, Vol. 1, No. 23, p. 1809.
[97] Article 25, *Ibid*.

Teacher Tenure in America and in Europe 137

SALARY AND PENSION PROVISIONS

Salary and pension protections for public school teachers are firmly established in European countries; but each of these safeguards exists as state regulations in only seven of the American states and the District of Columbia. Standardized schedules providing for graduated remuneration according to length of service exist by authority of law in five of the foreign countries and by common acceptance in the other (England and Wales). The common salary safeguard in the American states is the minimum salary schedule, which is found in Colorado, Indiana, Maryland, Massachusetts, New Jersey, New York, and Oregon.[98] A standardized schedule, similar to those of the foreign countries, is used by the District of Columbia. Protection against reduction of salary is afforded by the school laws of Colorado, the District of Columbia, Indiana, and New Jersey.

Five of the states listed above also have teacher pension laws, viz: Indiana, Maryland, Masachusetts, New Jersey, and New York; and the other two which have such laws are California and Wisconsin.[99] The pension law of the District of Columbia is one of the best in the United States.

SUMMARY

American indefinite tenure states differ considerably from the six European countries with regard to all matters included in this investigation except tenure status itself and disciplinary regulations; and even in the case of these exceptions noteworthy differences are apparent. The European countries have patently established more safeguards for the public schools and for the teaching profession, in the field of personnel regulations and practices, than have the American states. Centralized administration of schools in the foreign countries as opposed to local autonomy in this country is doubtless a major causative factor in the situation as it exists. But it also seems reasonable to suppose that the greater experience of the European countries with guaranteed tenure is

---

[98] "Is State Minimum Salary Schedule Needed?" *Ill. Teacher*, Vol. 18, pp. 314-18, May 1930.
[99] *Report of the Committee on Retirement Allowances of the N. E. A.*, June 1932, p. 47.

likewise an important factor. A list of the most important outcomes of the writer's comparative study follows.

1. Taken as a whole, the European countries require greater amounts of training for teaching, as measured in American college years, than do the American indefinite tenure states. There is not much difference in minimum requirements on the elementary level, but on the secondary level the disparity is marked.

2. In general, central authorities for education play an important part in the selection and appointment of elementary teachers abroad, and exercise almost complete control in the case of secondary teachers; whereas in the American states local authorities have complete control of selection and appointment of teachers. Competitive examinations are commonly used abroad to aid in the problem of selection, but are not employed by any states in this country.

3. Probationary requirements are similar as far as stipulated lengths of service are concerned and may even be termed lower for the European countries; however, it is much more difficult for the European than for the American teacher to attain permanent status. One reason for this difficulty is the existence of temporary or non-permanent positions, of other than the probationary type, in all the foreign countries except England and Wales.

4. Prevailing administrative organizations in the European countries make transfers much easier in theory, and to some extent in practice, than is the case in the American states. In this country, transfers within local systems may be difficult to effect and no transfers can be made among districts.

5. Tenure status itself differs but little, if any, in point of security; but the European teacher is often a civil servant and as such may have more prestige. Disciplinary regulations vary mainly in elaborateness of scales of penalties, some European countries having graduated scales of penalties which are stipulated by law.

6. All European countries have standardized salary schedules, providing for pay according to length of service, while only seven of the American states and the District of Columbia have any legal salary protections. Similarly, pension regulations are to be found in all the foreign countries and in but seven of the indefinite tenure states and the District of Columbia.

Teacher Tenure in America and in Europe 139

SELECTED REFERENCES

ALEXANDER, THOMAS. *The Training of Elementary Teachers in Germany.* Bureau of Publications, Teachers College, Columbia University, New York, 1927.
BOARD OF EDUCATION, ENGLAND. *Recent Educational Developments in Sweden.* Educational Pamphlets, No. 81. His Majesty's Stationery Office, London, 1930.
BORGESON, FRITHIOF CARL. *The Administration of Elementary and Secondary Education in Sweden.* Contributions to Education, No. 278. Bureau of Publications, Teachers College, Columbia University, New York, 1927.
COOK, KATHERINE M. *State Laws and Regulations Governing Teachers' Certificates.* United States Bureau of Education, Bulletin, 1927, No. 19, Washington, D. C.
De Høiere Almenskoler. A. W. Brøggers Boktrykkeris Forlag, Oslo, 1929.
DION, L. *Recueil Complet de la Législation de l'Enseignement Secondaire.* Papeterie Générale des Ecoles, 66 Rue Baudricourt, Paris, 1929.
IKIN, ALFRED E. *Organization and Administration of the Education Department.* Sir Isaac Pitman and Sons, Ltd., London, W.C. 1, 1931.
JENSEN, ARNE SIGURD. *The Rural Schools of Norway.* The Stratford Company, Boston, 1928.
KANDEL, I. L. *Comparative Education.* Houghton Mifflin Company, Boston, 1933.
—— (Translator). *French Elementary Schools: Official Courses of Study.* Bureau of Publications, Teachers College, Columbia University, New York, 1926.
KANDEL, I. L. and ALEXANDER, THOMAS (Translators). *The Reorganization of Education in Prussia.* Bureau of Publications, Teachers College, Columbia University, New York, 1927.
KILANDER, HOLGER F. *Science Education in the Secondary Schools of Sweden: A Comparative Study of Sweden and the United States.* Bureau of Publications, Teachers College, Columbia University, New York, 1931.
KÜHN, WALTER. *Schulrecht In Preussen.* Verlag Von B. G. Teubner, Leipzig-Berlin, 1926.
LANTENOIS, A. *Ce que l'Instituteur doit Savoir.* Librairie Classique Fernand Nathan, 16, Rue Des Fosses-Saint-Jacques, 16, Paris, 1930.
LOFTFIELD, GABRIEL E. *Secondary Education in Norway.* United States Office of Education, Bulletin, 1930, No. 17, Washington, D. C.
LONDON COUNTY COUNCIL. *Handbook Containing General Information with Reference to Teachers, Instructors, and Instructresses in London Public Elementary Schools.* P. S. King and Son, Ltd., London, 1927.
Lov om Folkeskolen I Kjøpstedene av 26 Juni 1889 (amended to July 1, 1927). Grøndahl & Søns Boktrykkeri, Oslo, 1928.
Lov om Folkeskolen Paa Landet av 26 Juni 1889 (amended to July 21, 1922). Grøndahl & Søns Boktrykkeri, Kristiania, 1923.
MCMURRY, RUTH E., MUELLER, MAX and ALEXANDER, THOMAS. *Modern*

Foreign Languages in France and Germany. Bureau of Publications, Teachers College, Columbia University, New York, 1930.
MINISTERO DELLA PUBBLICA ISTRUZIONE. *Bollettino Ufficiale.* Rome, July 7, 1923.
——. *Bollettino Ufficiale.* Rome, April 14, 1925.
——. *Regolamento Generale Sui Servizi Dell' Istruzione Elementare.* Provveditorato Generale Dello Stato Libreria, Rome, 1928.
——. *Testo Unico Delle Leggi E Delle Norme Giuridiche Sulla Istruzione Elementare, Post-Elementare E Sulle Sue Opere Di Integrazione.* Provveditorato Generale Dello Stato Libreria, Rome, 1928.
National Union of Teachers: Report for 1930. The "Schoolmaster" Publishing Company, Ltd., London, 1930.
OKTAVEC, FRANK L. *The Professional Education of Special Men Teachers of Physical Education in Prussia.* Contributions to Education, No. 369. Bureau of Publications, Teachers College, Columbia University, New York, 1929.
PERCY, LORD EUSTACE (Editor). *The Yearbook of Education, 1932.* Evans Brothers, Ltd., Montague House, Russell Square, London, W. C. 1, 1931.
RICHARD, C. *L'Enseignement en France.* Librairie Armand Colin, 103, Boulevard Saint-Michel, Paris, 1925.
Rundskrivelse fra Kirke—og Undervisningsdepartementet. No. 18 E. 1920 Jnr. 3557. 20. Oslo, Norway.
SELBY-BIGGE, SIR LEWIS AMHERST. *The Board of Education.* G. P. Putnam's Sons, Ltd., New York and London, 1927.
Skolväsendet I Tio Länder: En Översikt. Svensk Läraretidings Förlagsaktiebolag, Stockholm, 1931.
SOLEIL, JOSEPH. *Le Livre des Instituteurs.* Librairie H. Le Soudier, 174 et 176, Boulevard Saint-Germain, Paris, 1930.
WILSON, J. DOVER (Editor). *The Schools of England.* Sidgwick and Jackson, Ltd., London, 1928.

CHAPTER VII

Summary of Outcomes and Recommendations for Indefinite Tenure and Related Legislation

AT THE outset of this investigation, it was stated that the principle of indefinite tenure must be accepted or rejected on the basis of governmental policy or social philosophy. Either teachers play such an important rôle in the life of a nation, their need for a fair degree of independence in their work is so real, and their economic opportunities are so limited that they deserve protection in their positions or the opposite is the case. In the course of time, indefinite tenure should help to produce an improved teaching profession and thus better schools, but such results can only come gradually. The present study accepted protective tenure as a worthy element of social legislation, a practice which can best be defended on the ground that it is socially just. No attempt has been made to prove this position since it follows so closely those trends in modern social thought which hold that, generally speaking, present-day society provides too small a degree of economic security. Wherever applied, the principle of indefinite tenure remains the same; it is only the instruments of application that vary.

This investigation has isolated defects of laws and has demonstrated problems that arise under protective tenure statutes. Some of these problems belong peculiarly to indefinite tenure, while others are common to the field of personnel administration. A review of major findings will furnish an appropriate introduction for the recommendations which conclude this study.

SUMMARY

Viewed historically, indefinite tenure laws have come into being through the influence of professional organizations aided by the influence of the civil service. Most important of the professional organizations that have promoted the safeguarded tenure movement are the National Education Association, the American Federation of Teachers, and state teachers' associations; many others have been actively interested. Indefinite tenure can be likened to civil service on the score of protection, but in no case should be thought of as a merit system for teachers. Desire of teachers for security in office appears to have been the principal agent in bringing laws into being; nevertheless, there seems to have been a current belief that protection would in and of itself strengthen the profession and produce better schools. Proponents of indefinite tenure have from the beginning, therefore, claimed that their first allegiance is to the major aims of education.

Both the analysis and criterial evaluation of existing laws made in Chapter II of this study show that indefinite wording and incompleteness are outstanding characteristics of the statutes taken as a whole. Some laws, e.g., the California and Oregon statutes, err only slightly in these regards, but others are markedly deficient in both respects. In some cases omissions are compensated for by other provisions of the education law, which adequately cover the points in question. No moderating condition, however, was found in the case of the other common fault, that of poor phrasing or indefinite wording. Criteria used for judging the laws were developed by a survey of educational literature. These principles are inadequate in a number of instances, as was pointed out in connection with their development, but represent the best thought on the subject at the time a majority of the statutes were being enacted. Taken as a whole, the statutes rate only 60 per cent of perfect when measured by the criteria, the range being 38 to 81 per cent.

Operative effects of existing laws disprove a majority of the claims commonly made for indefinite tenure, reveal protection for teachers as the main value of the laws, and point to a number of problems which could be solved in part or in whole by carefully-framed, adequate indefinite tenure and related personnel statutes. Evidence that indefinite tenure is a stabilizing factor, that it makes the profession more attractive, and that it increases interest in professional improvement is so meager that no affirmative conclusion is warranted. The most that can be said at present is that it does not seem to have any adverse effect on these things. Dialectical reasoning leads to the conclusion that indefinite tenure should produce the above-named ends; yet since a number of factors influence results here it is doubtful whether measurement of the exact

Summary and Recommendations 143

effects of protected tenure will ever be possible. Problems emerging from the writer's study of operation now follow:

1. Wording of laws so as to obtain desired objectives and inclusion of all necessary provisions. This problem was emphasized by the analysis and evaluation and supported by the operative study.

2. Application of laws as to rural teachers. Two of the five states having statutes applying in rural districts, i.e., California and Indiana, have found that the rural teacher constitutes a separate and difficult problem. The inherent weakness of the Massachusetts law and the county unit organization of Maryland probably account for the non-existence of the problem in these states. New Jersey seems to have handled the rural problem rather well.

3. The probationary requirement, being inflexible at present, seems to work a hardship on some teachers, since school boards on occasion dismiss teachers merely to preclude their gaining permanent status. Furthermore, the trial period as usually administered is solely a testing and judging period rather than a period of training.

4. Dismissal of incompetent, inefficient, and otherwise undesirable teachers is a serious problem under any indefinite tenure statute. The gravity of this matter is indicated by the fact that in the city of Chicago, Illinois, from 1920 to 1931, inclusive, only fourteen teachers were dismissed and that from the dates of passage of the several state indefinite tenure laws through 1931, there occurred only 137 cases of appeal to higher educational and legal authorities. Causes given for dismissals in appeal cases are general, as a rule, and often overlap in meaning; they call for exercise of judgment on the part of ruling authorities.

5. Transfers and resignations are frequently inadequately provided for in protective tenure statutes or in other sections of the school code of a state. Both these devices are used, and appropriately in some instances, to avoid outright dismissal of teachers.

6. Downward revision of salary schedules is difficult under three state laws: the New Jersey statute decrees that reduction of individual salaries is tantamount to dismissal and the Colorado and Indiana laws make illegal anything but general reductions. It is also probable that the Minnesota and Wisconsin laws would present obstacles to downward revision; and salaries in the District of Columbia can be changed only by Congressional action.

7. The retirement problem takes on added significance under an indefinite tenure law, since without a pension law superannuated employees might insist on remaining in their positions after their usefulness had decreased considerably. The famous Armstrong case of Chicago illustrates this point. (See page 57 f.)

8. Miscellaneous problems include such matters as temporary suspension and the married woman teacher. Some of these problems should be cared for by indefinite tenure statutes and others should be left to administrative officials.

Comparison of important tenure and related personnel regulations and practices for six European countries, viz., England and Wales, France, Germany, Italy, Norway, and Sweden, and the American indefinite tenure states, shows marked similarity as regards tenure itself but considerable difference in the matter of safeguards for the profession and the schools, with the European systems having the advantage. Minimum training requirements for elementary teaching are about the same in the American states and in Europe, but requirements for the secondary level are much higher in Europe; central authorities and competitive examinations play a far greater part in the selection and appointment of European teachers; probationary requirements are no higher in Europe than in the American states, yet it is much more difficult to gain permanent status there, owing to flexible probationary periods and the existence of non-permanent positions in all countries except England and Wales; centralization of administration makes transfers easier in theory and to some extent in practice, in the European countries; tenure conditions in particular are about the same in the American states and the European countries, but the latter have more elaborate scales of disciplinary penalties; and, finally, all European countries have standardized salary schedules and pension provisions, whereas only five of the twelve American states and the District of Columbia have both these protections and each of two other pairs of states has one of the protections without the other.

RECOMMENDATIONS

Since indefinite tenure statutes proper do not exist apart from other education laws, it has been deemed advisable to treat first in this section the matter of related personnel provisions and organi-

Summary and Recommendations 145

zation practices. Without adequate laws covering the matters of units of administration, certification, pensions, and salaries an indefinite tenure law cannot function so as to protect satisfactorily the interests of teachers, pupils, and society. Recommendations for both auxiliary laws and for indefinite tenure statutes in particular were arrived at by a careful analysis of the results of the entire investigation; they are sufficiently general to be adaptable to specific situations and yet definite enough to be meaningful and helpful.

1. *Related Laws*

a. *Administrative Units*

Relatively large units of organization are necessary if best results are to be obtained from an indefinite tenure law. This principle is derived from the experiences of California and Indiana with laws applying to rural districts and from practices in certain European countries. That the difficulties of the two American states have been partly due to the size of the districts employed, there seems to be no doubt. It also seems obvious that the high degree of centralization in the European countries is contributing directly to the smooth functioning of indefinite tenure there. Where large units are used, there is much more opportunity for proper assignment of teachers and supervision of their work; furthermore, the situation is more conducive to the effecting of needed transfers and desired changes in organization practices. Leading educators in the United States have long been advocating the elimination of the small district or town unit and the substitution therefor of the county or some such larger unit, holding that the latter would be more efficient from both a financial and an educational standpoint. The tendency for some time has been toward increased centralization of control, but even yet a majority of the states in the Union do not have large enough units to warrant their adopting state-wide indefinite tenure laws.

What the size of a unit should be before the teachers therein become eligible for protection under an indefinite tenure statute, the writer will not essay to state definitely. Different geographical conditions and educational practices among the states warrant variations in the size of administrative units; however, it may be safely stated that no unit should be smaller than that of the average county in a Southern state. Criteria for determining the size of unit in any state should be administrative efficiency and educational desirability.

Some advantages would probably derive from having the state in charge of selection and appointment of teachers; but this appears visionary at present.

b. *Certification*

Stringent requirements for entrance upon teaching are essential if an indefinite tenure law is to operate so as to protect adequately the educational interests of society. It has been demonstrated in this study that practically all protective tenure laws now in force afford teachers a high degree of security once they have attained permanent status. Furthermore, it has been shown that teachers in American indefinite tenure states compare unfavorably, on the whole, with those of the more important European countries as regards training for their positions. If state-wide indefinite tenure laws should be enacted in the several American states at the present time, a large number of teachers with little more than a high school education and an overwhelmingly large number with no more than two years of college training would either be granted or made eligible for permanent status. There are only a few states in the country that have standards for certification sufficiently high to make safe and desirable state-wide practice of indefinite tenure. To accord teachers with low amounts of training permanent rank without making its continuance contingent upon further study, would in a sense jeopardize the future of the schools; for security in position, as has been pointed out in this study, does not alone increase professional study and interest. Consequently, it appears to be the part of wisdom to insist upon teachers being well trained before beginning teaching service.

c. *Retirement*

Provision for retirement of superannuated teachers should parallel or precede indefinite tenure legislation, otherwise schools may suffer from retention in office of teachers who have, as a result of age, become inefficient and incompetent. President Charles W. Eliot observed more than fifty years ago that "A regular provision for retiring old teachers on suitable annuities is a necessary supplement to a long-tenure system,"[1] and more recent writers have

[1] Eliot, Charles W., "Teachers' Tenure of Office"; In *Educational Reform*, p. 55.

Summary and Recommendations 147

expressed the same view. The unhappy experience of Chicago in attempting to retire teachers on part salary before the Miller act became operative illustrates well the close correlation between indefinite tenure and pension provisions. (See pages 57 f.)

The relationship just spoken of is not only administrative in character, but philosophical as well; for the social theory that upholds one practice also supports the other. Despite this fact, however, there are five states in the Union which have indefinite tenure laws without retirement statutes and six states which have retirement provisions alone. Evidently there is much yet to be done in the field of retirement legislation.

d. *Salaries*

Minimum salary laws or legal, graduated salary schedules should accompany indefinite tenure statutes. All European countries included in this study have standardized schedules; but only seven of the American indefinite tenure states and the District of Columbia have any form of legal salary protection. Fifteen other American states have some sort of legal regulation as to minimum salary, making the total for the country 22, or less than half of the states. Some form of salary protection is necessary if security in office is to carry with it the measure of economic security that is implied. Without such protection teachers are helpless if local boards decide to reduce salaries drastically as an economy measure or if they choose to use their absolute salary-determining power as a means of evading an indefinite tenure statute, i.e., by marked and unjustified reduction of salaries to force resignations. This does not mean that salary matters should be removed entirely from the jurisdiction of local boards; if these bodies have no power to reduce, difficult situations may arise such as the present one in New Jersey, where a mandatory salary provision makes impossible reduction of salaries, despite the fact that a considerable number of systems have not sufficient income to pay legal salaries. A salary law, therefore, should make provision for general reductions when necessary as well as provide reasonable protection for teachers.

2. *Indefinite Tenure Laws*

a. *General Recommendations*

Intelligent, clear, consistent wording is the first prerequisite of an indefinite tenure law, or, for that matter, of any law. Calcott[2]

[2] Calcott, Mary Stevenson, *Principles of Social Legislation*, pp. 22-23.

in a late treatise on social legislation observes that knowledge of existing laws and of judicial terms and devices for enforcement is essential to the drafting of any statute and quotes Luce as maintaining that "The framing of a statute is among the most difficult tasks that confront the intellect."[3] Since the technical part of legislation is so difficult and so pregnant with unfortunate possibilities, any professional organization, state department, or other group of persons who plan to propose an indefinite tenure bill before a state legislative body should engage the services of a competent lawyer for framing the proposed law. Educators should determine the content of a law, and this will doubtless vary from state to state, but the instrument itself should be devised by an expert in the field.

A second general suggestion, perhaps implied in the first, is that provision should be made regarding conflicting articles of law and for amending, revising, or otherwise changing the statute in question.

b. *Application to Districts*

An indefinite tenure statute should be made to apply only in districts sufficiently large to make possible efficient administration of personnel and progressive administration of all phases of school work. The need for reasonably large units was discussed in the preceding section and requires little elaboration here. Suffice it to say that many American states still maintain such small units of organization that it would be unwise for them to adopt state-wide indefinite tenure.

Optional application of a law in small districts might work satisfactorily in some states; however, as has been previously pointed out, it appears that no unit smaller than the average county or the city should be considered.

c. *Application to Employees*

The protection of an indefinite tenure law should be available to all educational employees whose chief concern is classroom instruction, that is, to all educational employees except those holding higher administrative posts. Common practice and prevailing opinion among educators both support the granting of protection to all properly certificated workers of the type named; but the

[3] Luce, Robert, *Legislative Procedure*, p. 566. Quoted in Calcott, *op. cit.*

Summary and Recommendations 149

writer feels that this is perhaps too all-inclusive. If protection were made available to all educational employees yet applicable only to those holding the higher grades of certificates, school interests would apparently be safeguarded to a greater degree than if no distinctions among certificates were made. This is suggested as a means of insuring better teaching, which does not seem to result automatically from the granting of protection.

High administrative officers, such as the superintendent of schools and his assistants, should not be granted permanent rank, except, perhaps, on the status of a teacher. Existing laws ordinarily do not give such officials protection and the best educational thought does not favor it, since to do so would be to bring in too great a risk of conservatism.

Provision should be made in a law for employees with service records of several years' duration in particular systems when the statute is enacted. Such employees either should be granted permanent status at once, or, better, should immediately become eligible for permanent status, or should be required to serve only a short trial period before becoming eligible for protection. Mere enactment of a law should in no case, however, carry with it automatic granting of protection to experienced employees.

It should also be provided that tenure of employees eligible for retirement should be at the will of the board. This is necessary to protect the system against employees whose usefulness has deteriorated on account of age.

If it is desired to protect school employees other than those of the educational, or instructional class, special laws can be devised for this purpose, as has been done in New Jersey and New York.

d. *Classification of Educational Employees*

Naturally, an indefinite tenure statute will classify all educational employees into at least two groups, i.e., permanent and nonpermanent. It should further classify non-permanent employees as probationers, substitutes, and temporary workers, provided the last two types of employees are used, and it seems that every large system should have such. As a rule, substitute teachers should be ineligible for permanent employment, owing to the uncertain nature of their work, but it might be well for the law to leave large systems which employ substitutes on regular salary free to grant such workers permanent status. The classification of temporary employees should certainly include all workers hired for indefinite or definite short periods, up to a fixed maximum. It might also include teachers who have completed legal probationary minimums without being promoted to permanent rank; for it will be proposed later that permanent rank not follow automatically the completion of a period of trial service. European school systems included in this study commonly maintain a non-permanent, or temporary classification, for experienced teachers, partly on account of economy, lower salaries being paid such employees; but evidence collected concerning this is not sufficient to warrant a recommendation that American states adopt the practice. The present California law provides that temporary employees become probationers upon completing sixty consecutive days of service. This appears to be a desirable provision if a permanent temporary classification is not to be maintained.

e. *Type of Tenure*

Tenure should be indefinite, or continuous, contingent upon efficient service and good behavior, for all educational workers who have been granted permanent status.

f. *Probationary Regulations*

A trial period should be stipulated with minimum and maximum lengths. The minimum, judging by common practice and the best educational thought on the subject, should be three years; the maximum might well be fixed at five or six years, but it is admitted that this is an arbitrary figure. It should not be possible for a school system to retain an employee who has completed the maximum probationary period without granting such employee permanent rank, unless the system has a temporary class of educational workers. The law should state the number of years, in the case of both the minimum and maximum, as school years or terms, since the use of calendar years gives school boards handle to evade the express intent of a protective tenure statute. Note should be made of the percentage amount of teaching service required during a given year for full credit. Place of service should be immaterial as long as it (the service) occurs within a given system; likewise, service in different types of positions should all count toward completion of a single probationary period. New teachers in a district who are not novitiates in teaching should be required

Summary and Recommendations 151

to serve only short periods of probation, not exceeding, say, one year in length. Provision should be made for unsatisfactory teachers to serve with more than one principal, and permanent rank should result only from definite board action.

School authorities should regard probation as a training period and not as a testing season. Perhaps no requirement to this effect should appear in law, but if probation is to serve its major purpose, it must be administered as stated.

g. *Disciplinary Regulations*

g-1. *Disciplinary Authority.* The local authority in charge of a school system should have complete control of disciplinary matters, except for appeals. This recommendation is in accord with existing legal provisions both in indefinite tenure states and in others, with legal decisions on the subject, and with the best principles of administration.

g-2. *Scale of Penalties.* Provision should be made for at least four penalties: (1) warning in the case of undesirable conduct or inefficiency; (2) temporary suspension pending trial on a grave charge, salary in such case during the suspension being dependent upon the outcome of the investigation; (3) temporary suspension with loss of salary followed by reinstatement, or resumption of service; and (4) complete dismissal from service. All of these except the first will be treated forthwith.

g-3. *Suspension.* As indicated above, suspension should be available as a protection for the school pending the outcome of an investigation of a serious charge for which dismissal would ordinarily be the penalty. Temporary suspension should also be allowed for minor indiscretions in the field of conduct. Practice in the United States does not favor this; but European practice does. It would enable school boards to discipline recalcitrant or careless employees without severing their relations with the system and thus jeopardizing their professional future; hence it should appeal both to boards and to teachers.

g-4. *Dismissal.* Causes which should be stipulated in law as justifying dismissal are: inefficiency, professional or physical incompetency, unbecoming personal conduct or unprofessional conduct, and persistent violation of or refusal to obey school laws or reasonable regulations for the government of schools. It would manifestly be impossible to include in a single statute all of the situations which might warrant dismissal, consequently relatively broad terms have been used which embrace all eventualities. Considerable leeway must be left the governing board in the determination of whether or not an offense justifies dismissal; however, specification of general causes is necessary if confusion and the probable abuse of board power are to be obviated.

h. *Disciplinary Procedure*

h-1. *Charges.* It should be required that charges against teachers be in writing and that they name general shortcomings, real or alleged. Ordinarily, only school officials will prefer charges, yet provision should be made for the filing of such by any interested party in the system, through the superintendent of schools. Provisions of indefinite tenure statutes now in force conform in the main to this requirement and the opinion of leading educators supports it. That all charges should be transmitted to the board by the superintendent seems obvious, since any other arrangement would be a violation of good administration.

h-2. *Hearings.* Provision should be made for the appearance of accused teachers before their respective boards, or special committees thereof, for hearings on charges, either as a matter of course or upon request. This idea is generally accepted as a principle of indefinite tenure legislation and has the support of prevailing practice. The hearing should be conducted in orderly fashion, in the general manner of a law trial, with both parties privileged to use witnesses and counsel. Details of hearings should, however, be left to local boards and should be prescribed in board rules. No evidence has been adduced which indicates that a private is better than an open hearing, therefore this matter should as yet be left to local boards.

h-3. *Notices.* The nature of notices in regard to charges, hearings, and decisions of disciplinary authorities should be stipulated in law. Time limits may well vary, but it seems that all notices should be in writing and should be delivered either in person or by registered mail.

i. *Appeals*

To protect teachers against boards unfriendly to indefinite tenure, against personal antagonism, or misapplication of a law, definite provision should be made for appeal from decisions to

Summary and Recommendations 153

state educational authorities and to the law courts. The general right of appeal has long been recognized, still some leading educators have argued that the only recourse should be to educational authorities. Data presented in this study relative to appeals decided by courts of law indicate no marked bias in favor of either teachers or local boards. Claims of local boards have been upheld more often than those of teachers; but the trend has not been strong enough to invite abuse of discretionary power. The order of appeal should be first to educational authorities and then to legal tribunals.

j. *Transfers*

Transfers within districts without loss of tenure status should be provided for, such transfers involving either promotion or demotion. A provision of this type would simplify transfers and would preclude the possibility of salary disputes. It also appears that transfers among districts, either voluntarily or at the instance of governing boards with the teachers consenting, should be possible without the complete loss by employees of accrued tenure protection. A short probationary period might be required in the new system, during which time the teacher might be free to return to the district of origin, either as an active employee or with the assurance of preference in assignment when vacancies in her field occur. Provisions of the type defined are common in Europe, where highly centralized systems of education are the rule, but no American states or other governmental units have yet attempted such.

k. *Resignations*

Every school code should, of course, make provision for the resignation of teachers, as a protection to local boards and the schools; and the proper place for this seems to be in the tenure section. This provision should stipulate the number of days' notice required—which should at least be thirty—, that the notice be in writing, and the type of action required of the board for resignation to become effective.

l. *Salaries*

If an adequate salary law is on the statute books, no mention of salaries should be made in the indefinite tenure law. But in case a salary provision is made, it should do nothing more than limit reductions to those of a general character, except in the case of transfers, when teachers should receive in their new positions salaries that are common to workers of the same class.

m. *In-Service Training*

Whether or not this matter should be touched upon by an indefinite tenure law is a matter of conjecture. It seems to the writer that some legal requirement is necessary and that the proper place for it is in the certification law rather than in the indefinite tenure statute.

CONCLUSION

The suggestions of this chapter once crystallized into law should provide an effective instrument for protecting teachers in their positions and at the same time for assuring children and society in general that their educational interests will be adequately safeguarded. It should be remembered, however, that no law, regardless of how perfectly framed, could alone produce the desired results. Wise interpretation and application of an indefinite tenure statute and of all other educational laws, in short, good school administration, can do more than anything else to make indefinite tenure function in practice so as to promote the good of all concerned.

GENERAL BIBLIOGRAPHY

ADERHOLD, R. T. "The Influence of the N. E. A. on Tenure." *Georgia Education Journal*, 21:21-22, December 1928.

ALLEN, I. M. *The Teacher's Contractual Status.* Contributions to Education, No. 304. Bureau of Publications, Teachers College, Columbia University, New York, 1928.

ALLTUCKER, MARGARET M. "Tenure in Present Positions and Training of City School Superintendents." *School and Society*, 29:649-52, May 18, 1929.

ALMACK, J. C. "The Problem of Teacher Tenure." *American School Board Journal*, 63:29-30, November 1921.

ALMACK, J. C. and LANG, A. R. *Problems of the Teaching Profession*, pp. 215-34. Houghton Mifflin Company, Boston, 1925.

ANDERSON, EARL W. *The Teacher's Contract and Other Legal Phases of Teacher Status.* Contributions to Education, No. 246. Bureau of Publications, Teachers College, Columbia University, New York, 1927.

BAKER, B. R. "Lack of Tenure of Office a Factor in School Expenses." *American School Board Journal*, 72:48, May 1926.

BARDY, JOSEPH. "Tenure Laws in the United States." *University of Pennsylvania Ninth Annual Schoolmen's Week Proceedings*, 1922, pp. 215-20.

BENEDICT, ERNEST M. "Indefinite Tenure of Office for Teachers." *American School Board Journal*, 60:85-86, 89, January 1920.

BESSAC, HARRY. "How the Tenure Law is Working." *Sierra Educational News*, 24:16, December 1928.

BOYNTON, F. D. "The Effects of Tenure and Compulsory Salary Increment Laws." *Journal of New York State Teachers' Association*, 6:249-55, November 13, 1919.

BROOME, E. C. "Advantages and Disadvantages of the Permanent Tenure Law in New Jersey." *University of Pennsylvania Ninth Annual Schoolmen's Week Proceedings*, 1922, pp. 226-27.

CARR, WILLIAM G. "Teacher Tenure in California." *Sierra Educational News*, 24:21-24, September 1928.

CLARK, C. L. *The Tenure of Teachers in the Profession, With Special Reference to Wisconsin.* Alumni Press, University of Michigan, 1928.

COPE, A. B. "The Indiana Teacher Tenure Law." *Co-operative School Bulletin*, 6:14-15, March 1928.

CRABTREE, J. W. "The Principles of Teacher Tenure." *Nebraska Educational Journal*, 6:525, December 1926.

CUBBERLEY, ELLWOOD P. *Public School Administration*, pp. 317-38. Houghton Mifflin Company, Boston, 1929.

———. *State School Administration*, pp. 642-68. Houghton Mifflin Company, Boston, 1927.

EDITORIAL. "Higher Standards and the Tenure Problem." *American School Board Journal*, 77:70, July 1928.

EDITORIAL. "The Introductory Stages of Teacher Tenure." *American School Board Journal*, 77:66, October 1928.

EDITORIAL. "Indiana Contests Teacher-Tenure Law." *American School Board Journal*, 77:124, November 1928.

EDITORIAL. "Teacher Tenure." *American Teacher*, October 1926.

EDITORIAL. "The Effect of Permanent Tenure upon School Efficiency." *Educational Review*, 66:285-86, December 1923.

EDITORIAL. "Why Indiana Needs Tenure." *Indiana Teacher*, 71:16, January 1927.

EDITORIAL. "What Other States Think of Tenure Law." *Indiana Teacher*, 71:14-15, April 1927.

EDITORIAL. "A Victory for Teachers." *Indiana Teacher*, 75:14, February 1931.

EDITORIAL. "The Teacher Tenure Law." *Indiana Teacher*, 76:15, December 1931.

EDITORIAL. "Tenure Problems." *Pennsylvania School Journal*, 75:153, November 1926.

EDWARDS, I. N. "Marriage as a Legal Cause for Dismissal of Women Teachers." *Elementary School Journal*, 25:692, May 1925.

ELIOT, CHARLES W. *Educational Reform*, pp. 49-58. The Century Co., New York, 1905.

ELSBREE, W. S. *Teacher Turnover in Cities and Villages of New York State*. Contributions to Education, No. 300. Bureau of Publications, Teachers College, Columbia University, New York, 1928.

EYLER, A. L. "The Achievements of Teacher Tenure." *Ohio Schools*, 6:299, 302, October 1928.

FERGUSON, JAMES. "The Tenure of Teachers." *National Education Association Addresses and Proceedings*, 1920, 58:158-60.

GLOVER, H. B. "Tenure and the California Teachers' Association." *Southwestern Classroom Teacher*, 1:12-13, May 29, 1930.

GOODELL, GEORGE S. "Does Society Need More State Teacher-Tenure Laws?" *Journal of Educational Sociology*, 1:503-04, April 1928.

GRAYBIEL, J. M. "Tenure for Teachers." *American Teacher*, 16:5, 11, March 1932.

HOLMSTEDT, RALEIGH W. *A Study of the Effects of the Teacher Tenure Law in New Jersey*. Contributions to Education, No. 526. Bureau of Publications, Teachers College, Columbia University, New York, 1932.

HOSMAN, E. M. "The Rural Teacher; Tenure." *Nebraska Educational Journal*, 6:536-37, December 1926.

HOUSMAN, IDA E. "High Spots in Framing a Tenure Law." *American School Board Journal*, 70:37-39, March 1925.

———. "Tenure Once More." *Educational Review*, 68:118-22, October 1924.

HUNTER, FRED M. "Teacher Tenure in the United States." *National Education Association Addresses and Proceedings*, 1926, 64:202-20; 1927, 65:208-35.

Bibliography

———. "What Leading Educators Say About Tenure for Teachers." *Bulletin of the Class Room Teachers' Association*, 14:10-13, January 1927.
JOHNSON, RUTH M. "Permanent Tenure for Rural Teachers." *New York State Education*, 14:443, March 1927.
KANDEL, I. L. "Tenure of Service for Teachers." *Teachers College Record*, 26:127-44, 197-204, October and November 1924.
LEWIS, E. E. *Personnel Problems of the Teaching Staff*, pp. 328-41; 342-52. The Century Co., New York, 1925.
LUCKIE, W. V. "Teacher Tenure Laws in Other States." *Alabama School Journal*, 47:16, January 1930.
MILLER, MABEL E. "Tenure of Office of Teachers in Colorado." *Colorado School Journal*, 42:22, September 1926.
MORGAN, JOY E. "Principles of Tenure." *Indiana Teacher*, 72:13-14, February 1928.
NATIONAL EDUCATION ASSOCIATION. "The Tenure of Office of the Superintendent of Schools." *First Yearbook of the Department of Superintendence*, 1:110-22, 1923.
———. "Facts on State Educational Needs." *Research Bulletin*, 1:54-57, January 1923.
———. "The Problem of Teacher Tenure." *Research Bulletin*, Vol. 2, No. 5, November 1924.
PARKINSON, WILLIAM D. "Teacher's Tenure." *Journal of Education*, 79:115-16, January 29, 1914.
ROWLAND, ALBERT LINDSAY. "An Adequate Tenure Law for the Teachers of Pennsylvania." *Pennsylvania School Journal*, 75:383-85, February 1927.
SCATTERGOOD, MRS. JOSEPH. "Teacher Tenure from the School Director's Viewpoint." *American School Board Journal*, 78:130, May 1929.
STILLMAN, CHARLES B. "Tenure of Position of Superintendents and Teachers." *American Teacher*, 6:34-37, March 1917.
THIEL, RICHARD B. "Legal Phases of Teacher Selection, Tenure, and Dismissal." *Nation's Schools*, 1:45-48, June 1928.
VANATTA, HARRY E. "A Study of Existing and Proposed State Tenure Laws for Teachers." Unpublished Master's Thesis, University of Pittsburgh, 1924.
WISEHART, ROY P. "Some Phases of Teacher Tenure in Indiana." *Indiana University Proceedings of the High School Principals' Conference, 1927.* Indiana University Bulletin, 4:45-48, March 1928.

APPENDIX

A

Appeal Cases That Have Arisen under Existing Indefinite Teacher Tenure Laws Listed According to Type[1]

INEFFICIENCY, INCOMPETENCY, UNPROFESSIONAL AND UNBECOMING CONDUCT, AND REFUSAL TO COÖPERATE[2]

Alexander v. Manton Joint Union Sch. Dist., 73 Cal. App. 252, 238 P. 742, 255 P. 516 (1927).
Blackus v. Bd. of Ed. of Delaware Twp., N.J.S.R., 1912, 122.
Coles v. Bd. of Ed. of Pilesgrove Twp., N.J.S.R., 1912, 95; N.J.S.L.D. 1928, 172 (1911).
Conrow v. Bd. of Ed. of Lumberton Twp., N.J.S.R., Vol. 1, 1913, 231; N.J.S.L.D., 1928, 185 (1914).
Corrigan v. Sch. Committee of New Bedford, 250 Mass. 334 (1924).
Matter of Appeal of Culver, 37 N.Y.S.D.R. 140 (1926).
Davis v. Bd. of Ed. of Overpeck Twp., N.J.S.R., 1916, 209.
Duffey v. Sch. Committee of Hopkinton, 236 Mass. 5, 127 N.E. 540 (1920).
Fitch v. Bd. of Ed. of South Amboy, N.J.S.R., 1913, 249; N.J.S.L.D., 1928, 173 (1914).
Matter of Appeal of Fotheringham, 15 N.Y.S.D.R. 498 (1918).
Fountain v. Bd. of Ed. of Madison Twp., N.J.S.R., 1917, 298; N.J.S.L.D., 1928, 179.
Gammon v. Bd. of Ed. of Leonia, N.J.S.R., 1921, 310.
Goldsmith v. Bd. of Ed. of Sacramento City H. S. Dist. et al., 66 Cal. App. 157, 255 P. 783 (1924).
Hamilton v. Bd. of Ed. of Irvington, N.J.S.R., 1929, 860.
Lachmund v. Bd. of Ed. of Bergenfield, N.J. In Ms. (1921).
Leistner v. Bd. of Ed. of Landis Twp., N.J.S.R., 1927, 118; N.J.S.L.D., 1928, 130 (1926).
Marstellar v. Bd. of Ed. of Pleasantville, N.J.S.R., Vol. 1, 1913, 246; N.J.S.L.D., 1921, 530.
McCain and McCain v. Bd. of Ed. of Harrison, N.J.S.R., 1915, 50.
MacDonald v. Bd. of Ed. of Hamilton Twp., N.J.S.L.D., 1921, 499 (1917).

[1] This appendix contains all appeal cases, with complete references, that had been decided by state educational authorities and higher legal tribunals through December 1931. The date of each final decision appears either as a part of the citation or in parentheses at the close.

[2] All cases in this category involved two or more of the charges specified except four, in each of which a single charge was preferred.

McDowell v. Bd. of Ed. of New York, 104 N.Y.M.R. 564, 172 N.Y.S. 590 (1918).
Matter of Appeal of Morton, 39 N.Y.S.D.R., 9 (1929).
Matter of Appeal of Pignol. 21 N.Y.S.D.R., 270 (1919).
Matter of Appeal of Pratt, 25 N.Y.S.D.R., 65 (1921).
Saxton v. Bd. of Ed. of Los Angeles City Sch. Dist. et al., 77 Cal. Dec. 493, 206 Cal. 758, 276 P. 998 (1929).
Matter of Appeal of Shea and Foody, 26 N.Y.S.D.R., 469 (1921).
Wallace v. Bd. of Ed. of Greenwich Twp., N. J., *Ed. Bul.*, April 1931, 670.
Weekley v. Bd. of Ed. of Teaneck Twp., N.J. In Ms. (1929).
Van Horn v. Bd. of Ed. of Hope Twp., N.J. In Ms. (1922).

SUMMARY DISMISSAL

Anderson v. Scranton et al., Cal. 295 P. 544 (1931).
Barhite v. Bd. of Ed. of West New York, N.J.S.R., 1913, 221; 86 N.J.L. 674; 92 A. 92 (1914).
Bland v. Bd. of Trustees of Galt Joint Union H. S. Dist. et al., 67 Cal. App. 784, 228 P. 395 (1924).
Clark v. Bd. of Ed. of Eureka Sch. Dist. et al., 64 Cal. App. 757, 222 P 854 (1923).
Clayton (or Sumner) v. Bd. of Ed. of Orange, N.J.S.R., Vol. 1, 1913, 233; N.J.S.L.D., 1928, 195 (1914).
Conrow v. Bd. of Ed. of Lumberton Twp., N.J.S.R., 1912, 134; N.J.S.L.D., 1928, 184.
Francis v. Walker et al., 63 Cal. App. Dec. 1166, 293 P. 808 (1930).
Grigsby v. King et al., 74 Cal. Dec. 439, 202 Cal. 299, 260 P. 789 (1927).
Matter of Appeal of Healy, 34 N.Y.S.D.R., 449 (1926).
LaShells v. Hench et al., 98 Cal. App. 6, 58 Cal. App. Dec. 1128, 276 P. 377 (1929).
Marstellar v. Bd. of Ed. of Pleasantville, N.J.S.R., 1912, 104 N.J.S.L.D., 1921, 525.
McCurdy v. Bd. of Ed. of Matawan, N.J.S.R., 1927, 55; N.J.S.L.D., 1928, 134.
Pistor v. Bd. of Ed. of Secaucus, N.J.S.R., 1929, 104.
State ex rel. Nyberg v. Bd. of Ed. of Milwaukee et al., Wis., 209 N.W. 683 (1926).
Tomlin v. Bd. of Ed. of Glassboro, 1 N.J.M.R. 568 (1923).
U. S. ex rel. Cardozo v. Baird et al., 35 W.L.R. 15, 30 App. D.C. 86 (1906).
U. S. ex rel. Nalle v Hoover, 31 App. D.C. 311, 35 W.L.R., 371 (1908).

NON-RETENTION PROBATIONARY TEACHERS

Ackerman v. Bd. of Ed. of Phillipsburg, N.J.S.R., 1926, 78.
Allen v. Bd. of Ed. of Belleville, N.J. Sup. Dec., 1932, 827 (1928).
Blalock v. Ridgway et al., 92 Cal. App. 132, 56 Cal. App. Dec. 477, 267 P. 713 (1928).
Brandes v. Bd. of Ed. of Hoboken, N.J.S.L.D., 1921, 550 (1913).
Carrol v. St. Bd. of Ed., 8 N.J.M.R., 859, 152 A. 339 (1930).

Appendix

Matter of Appeal of Crum, MacLellan, Pratt, Sill, and Taylor, 20 N.Y.S.D.R., 195 (1919).
Matter of Appeal of Fayette, 21 N.Y.S.D.R., 330 (1919).
Fleming v. Bd. of Trustees of Oakville Sch. Dist., 64 Cal. App. Dec. 795, 296 P. 925 (1931).
Gamnon v. Bd. of Ed. of Elizabeth, N.J.S.R., 1924, 251.
Goble v. Bd. of Ed. of Easthampton Twp., N.J.S.R., 1927, 70; N.J.S.L.D., 1928, 86 (1926).
Holm v. Bd. of Ed. of Rochester, 252 N.Y.S. 389, 141 N.Y.M.R. 194 (1931).
Matter of Appeal of Krebs, 26 N.Y.S.D.R. 353 (1921).
Matter of Appeal of Mandigo, 35 N.Y.S.D.R., 633 (1926).
O'Connor v. Emerson et al., 188 N.Y.S. 236, 196 App. Div. 807; affirming order (1920) 185 N.Y.S. 49, 113 N.Y.M.R. 472; order affirmed 134 N.E. 572, 232 N.Y. 561 (1921).
Ostergren v. Bd. of Ed. of Hoboken, N.J.S.R., 1926, 60.
Owens v. Bd. of Ed. of the City of Santa Cruz, et al., 68 Cal. App. 403, 229 P. 881 (1924).
Shapiro v. Bd. of Ed. of Paterson, N.J.S.R., 1925, 247; 3 N.J.M.R. 406.

ABOLITION OF POSITION

Cowperthwaite v. Bd. of Ed. of Medford, N.J. In Ms. (1922).
Matter of Appeal of Etz, 32 N.Y.S.D.R. 169 (1924).
Fitzherbert v. Bd. of Ed. of Roxbury Twp., N.J.S.R., 1916, 193; N.J.S.L.D., 1928, 200.
Funston v. Sch. Dist. No. 1, Or., 278 P. 1075, 63 A.L.R. 1410 (1929).
Gordon v. Bd. of Ed. of Jefferson Twp., N.J.S.R., 1924, 250; N.J.S.L.D., 1928, 169 (1924).
Kinney v. Bd. of Ed. of Trenton, N.J.S.R., 1925, 266 (1924).
Kuyl v. Bd. of Ed. of Paterson, N.J.S.R., 1925, 288; N.J.S.L.D., 1928, 182.
Matter of Appeal of Mack, 30 N.Y.S.D.R. 154 (1923).
Mills v. Bd. of Ed. of Washington Twp., N.J. In Ms. (1929).
Osborne v. Bd. of Ed. of Passaic Twp., N.J. In Ms. (1923).
Pollard v. Sch. Committee of Revere, 249 Mass. 525, 144 N.E. 377 (1924).
Sweeney v. Sch. Committee of Revere, 249 Mass. 525, 144 N.E. 377 (1924).
Tobey v. Bd. of Ed. of Newark, N.J.S.L.D., 1928, 161 (1914).
Wisner v. Bd. of Ed. of Neptune Twp., N.J.S.R., 1929, 873.

TRANSFER QUESTIONS

Alexander v. Sch. Dist. No. 1, 84 Or. 172, 164 P. 711 (1917).
Boody v. School Committee of Barnstable, Mass. 177 N.E. 78 (1931).
Matter of Appeal of Callahan, 32 N.Y.S.D.R. 162 (1924).
Cassiday v. Bd. of Ed. of Jersey City, N.J. In Ms. (1931).
Davis v. Bd. of Ed. of Overpeck Twp., N.J.S.R., 1912, 128; N.J.S.R., 1913, 235; N.J.S.L.D., 1928, 187, 295 (1913).
Matter of Appeal of Kiernan, 36 N.Y.S.D.R. 140 (1926).
Matter of Appeal of Livingston, 37 N.Y.S.D.R. 684 (1928).

162 Indefinite Teacher Tenure

MacNeal v. Bd. of Ed. of Ocean City, N.J.S.R., 1928, 41; N.J.S.L.D., 1928, 152.
Morrison v. Bd. of Ed. of Delaware Twp., N.J.S.R., 1915, 59; N.J.S.L.D., 1928, 163.
Munson v. Bd. of Ed. of Ringwood Borough, N.J. In Ms. (1922).
Myers v. Bd. of Ed. of Readington Twp., N.J.S.R., 1918, 196.
Noonan and Arnot v. Bd. of Ed. of Paterson, N.J.S.R., 1925, 277; N.J.S.L.D., 1928, 116.
Shroder v. Bd. of Ed. of Irvington, N.J.S.R., 1919, 216.

MARRIAGE OF WOMEN TEACHERS

Matter of Appeal of Bennett. Md. In Ms. (1931).
Blair v. U. S. ex rel. Hellmann, 44 W.L.R. 386, 45 App. D.C. 353 (1916).
Dutart v. Woodward et al., 99 Cal. App. 736, 279 P. 493 (1929).
Nommensen v. Bd. of Ed. of Hoboken, N.J.S.L.D., 1928, 166 (1923).
Richards v. Sch. Dist. No. 1, 78 Or. 621, 153 P. 482; L.R.A. 1916 C. 789; Ann. Cas. 1917 D, 266 (1915).
Sheldon v. Sch. Committee of Hopedale, Mass. 177 N.E. 94 (1931).
Matter of Appeal of Thomas, 33 N.Y.S.D.R., 12 (1925).
State ex rel. Thompson v. Bd. of Sch. Directors of Milwaukee, 191 N.W. 746, 179 Wis. 284 (1923).

REDUCTION OF SALARY

Fidler v. Bd. of Trustees of Roseville Union H. S., 64 Cal. App. Dec. 851, 296 P. 912 (1931).
Gowdy v. St. Bd. of Ed. of N. J. et al., (and Homer v. Same), 84 N.J.L. 231, 86 A. 948; Affirmed 85 N.J.L. 726, 89 A. 1135 (1913).
Morgenweck et al. v. Bd. of Ed. of Gloucester City, N. J. In Ms. (1930).
Paquette v. City of Fall River, Mass. 179 N.E. 588 (1931).
Reed and Hills v. Bd. of Ed. of Trenton, N.J.S.R., 1917, 309; N.J.S.L.D. 148 (1918).
Samuelsen v. Bd. of Ed. of Edgewater, N.J., Ed. Bul., Vol. 18, No. 4, Dec. 1931, 237.
Wakefield v. Bd. of Ed. of Hoboken, N.J.S.R., 1914, 118; N.J.S.L.D., 1928, 146.

UNBECOMING CONDUCT

Craze v. Bd. of Ed. of Allendale, N.J., Sup. Dec. 1931, 881 (1930).
Johnson v. Bd. of Ed. of Stafford Twp., N.J.S.R., 1912, 125
Oliver v. Bd. of Ed. of Hoboken, N.J.S.R., 1917, 305; N.J.S.L.D., 1928, 128.
Matter of Appeal of Mufson, Schneer, and Schmalhausen, 18 N.Y.S.D.R. 393 (1918).
Smith v. Bd. of Ed. of Phillipsburg, N.J.S.R., 1917, 313; N.J.S.L.D., 1928, 132 (1918).

SUITS FOR LOST SALARY

Bronson v. Bd. of Ed. of Binghamton, 136 N.Y.M.R. 76, 240 N.Y.S. 291 (1930).

Appendix

Martin v. Fisher et al., 108 Cal. App. 34, 63 Cal. App. Dec. 57, 293 P. 808 (1930).
Oxman v. Independent Sch. Dist. of Duluth, Minn., 227 N.W. 351 (1929).
Matter of Appeal of Wade, 40 N.Y.S.D.R. 44 (1930).

INSUBORDINATION

Cheesman v. Bd. of Ed. of Gloucester City, N.J.S.L.D., 1928, 156; 1 N.J.M.R. 318 (1923).
Gebhart v. Bd. of Ed. of Hopewell, N.J.S.R., 1928, 48.
Welch v. Bd. of Ed. of West Orange, N.J.S.L.D., 1928, 197 (1914).

QUESTION OF CERTIFICATE

Bagnell v. Bd. of Ed. of Bayonne, N.J.S.R., 1915, 61.
Levitch v. Bd. of Ed. of New York, 209 N.Y.S. 271, 212 N.Y. App. 598; reversed 215 N.Y.S. 309, 216 N.Y. App. 391; original order affirmed 243 N.Y. 373, 153 N.E. 495 (1926).
McAuley v. Bd. of Ed. of Prospect Park, N.J.S.R., 1916, 189; N.J.S.L.D., 1928, 210 (1916).

INELIGIBLE SCHOOL EMPLOYEES

Lamarsh v. Sch. Committee of Chicopee, Mass. 172 N.E. 117 (1930).
Ryan v. Sch. Dist. No. 26, Arapahoe Co., Colo., 270 P. 865 (1928).
Waters v. Bd. of Ed. of Newark, N. J. In Ms. (1931).

MISCELLANEOUS[3]

Anderson v. Scranton et al., Cal., 295 P. 544 (1931).
Armstrong et al. v. City of Chicago et al., 247 Ill. App. 584, 159 N.E. 217 (1928).
Matter of Appeal of Boyd, 40 N.Y.S.D.R. 248 (1931).
Clifford v. Sch. Committee of Lynn, Mass., 175 N.E. 634 (1931).
Conway v. Bd. of Ed. of Edgewater, N.J.S.R., 1928, 101.
Davis v. Bd. of Ed. of Boonton, N.J.S.L.D., 1928, 141 (1925).
Nicholson v. Bd. of Ed. of Swedesboro, N.J.S.R., 1912, 96; 83 A. 488, 83 N.J.L. 36.
Pearce et al. v. Burns and the Bd. of Ed. of Gloucester City, N.J. In Ms. (1923).
Matter of Appeal of Pietsch, 38 N.Y.S.D.R. 17 (1928).
Rein v. Bd. of Ed. of Riverside Twp., N.J. In Ms. (1931).
Schermerhorn v. Bd. of Ed. of Hanover Twp., N.J.S.R., 1920, 192.
Shaver v. Bd. of Ed. of Avalon, N.J.S.R, 1927, 46.
Taggart v. Sch. Dist. No. 1, 96 Or. 422, 188 P. 1119 (1920).
White v. Bd. of Ed. of Hillsdale, N.J.S.R., 1927, 63; N.J.S.L.D., 1928, 124 (1926).
White v. Bd. of Ed. of Readington, N.J.S.R., 1927, 87.

[3] No more than two cases of any one type are included in this classification, which comprises questions of resignation, forced leaves of absence, suspensions, etc.

APPENDIX

B

Abbreviations for Legal Sources

A.—Atlantic
A. L. R.—American Law Reports
App. D. C.—Appellata Reports, District of Columbia
Ann. Cas.—Annotated Cases
Cal.—California Reports
Cal. App.—California Appeal Reports
Cal. App. Dec.—California Appeal Decisions
Cal. Decisions—California Reports
F.—Federal Reporter
Ill. App.—Illinois Appeal Reports
L. R. A.—Lawyers' Reports Annotated
Mass.—Massachusetts Reports
N. J. L.—New Jersey Law Reports
N. J. M. R.—New Jersey Miscellaneous Reports
N. Y.—New York Reports
N. Y. App.—New York Appeal Reports
N. Y. M. R.—New York Miscellaneous Reports
N. Y. S.—New York Supplement Reports
N. E.—Northeastern Reporter
N. W.—Northwestern Reporter
Or.—Oregon Reports
P.—Pacific Reporter
N. J. S. L. D.—New Jersey School Law Decisions
N. J. Sup. Dec.—Supplement to School Law Decisions, New Jersey
N. J. S. R.—Annual Report of the State Board of Education and of the Commissioner of Education, New Jersey
N. Y. S. D. R.—Annual Report of the State Department of Education, New York
Wis.—Wisconsin Reports
W. L. R.—Western Law Reports